He Talks With Me

A Diary of Answered Prayers

Received by
Billie Steves

DREAM STREET PUBLISHING
Tucson, Arizona

Book design by Del Kyger
Cover photograph by
Opal Westmoreland & Lisa Kedro
Cover design by Judy Miller
Interior drawings by Barbara Eagan

20 15 10 9 8 7 6 5 4 3 2 1

For information, write or call:

DREAM STREET PUBLISHING
P.O. Box 19028
Tucson, Arizona 85731-9028
(520)733-9695

If you are unable to order this book from your local
bookseller, you may order directly from the publisher.
Quantity discounts for organizations are available.
Order Toll Free, 1-800-795-1513

ISBN 0-9665097-0-6

Printed in Canada

Dedicated

*To all those who want to know, and be
One with God.*

Preface

I AM THAT I AM. These words are the most remembered from Cecil B. DeMille's *The Ten Commandments*. I always thought that these words referred only to God. However, after fifty years of being a channel for God's messages, I now realize that we are all the "I AM" that is One with the All.

I AM represents the essence of Spirit that we all share. God is asking us to relinquish the I of individuality for the collective I AM and ascend to His Kingdom and surrender to the work of our Father, first and above all else. I AM THAT I AM is the essence of our soul experience in the embodiment of light. We are One with the Spirit of God.

In God's answers to my prayers, He repeatedly emphasizes that He loves us all equally because we are all One in Spirit. All of us are the living enterprise of God, having been created (spiritually) in His image. He tells us that we are all extensions of God Spirit, and we all have the ability to co-create with God.

The underlying message of God's words all these

years is for us to take responsibility for the world we have created. I learned that if I am not happy with the way things are going in my life, then I have the ability and the responsibility to change my life. Spirit has taught me that all I have to do is express my desire for change. All that remains is to Let Go And Let God do the rest. It works! I speak from personal experience. All we have to do is turn our challenges and problems over to God knowing that they will be solved in a manner that results in the highest good for all concerned.

God's answers to my prayers have helped me to realize that we must believe we are worthy of His gifts and that we are always safely cradled in His arms. All we are asked to do is to trust that God will carry us through all the obstacles, and know that we are loved and we are in the perfect place at this moment in time. God asks that we live in the NOW and not in the past or the future. We're asked to "just be" and God will do the rest.

Searching for Truth, for more illumination concerning Reality and my true Self has been the common denominator in my life since I was sixteen years old. It was then that I experienced a "miraculous" outpouring of divine Principle.

I was a sophomore in high school. As a homework assignment in my geometry class, we were asked to prove a theorem using only our textbook and notes. We could not solicit any help from parents, siblings or friends. I spent the entire evening attempting to develop the proof, but to no avail. Finally after hours of frustration, I went to bed and prayed to Spirit to provide me with the solution.

In the middle of the night I awoke with the image of a formula in my mind's eye. By the light in the hallway, I wrote down the formula and went back to sleep. I arose the next morning and immediately tested the solution and it was correct, although I hadn't a clue as to how to derive it. When Miss Conkey asked for the answer, the smartest boy in the class and I raised our hands. Both of us were asked for the formula and both of us had the correct answer.

Much to my embarrassment, I was asked to go to the board and illustrate the solution. I told Miss Conkey that I could not because the formula came to me as an answer to my prayer and I had no idea how to prove it. I was so grateful that Miss Conkey believed me. In fact, she said she had heard of such happenings and believed it was divine inspiration. The other student was asked to illustrate the proof, which he did, taking the entire period and all the chalk boards in the classroom.

God answering my prayer has had a profound and lasting effect on my life. This experience proved to me that there *is* a Power within all of us that can help us solve *all* problems if we would only ask, and then remain open for the answer. It is this same power that helps us to be at peace and to see life and the world around us as the beautiful experiences they are meant to be. From that day on, I knew I was not alone in this life. Spirit was at my side all the time... guiding, directing, answering my prayers and meeting my needs.

One morning about fifty years ago, while alone and being quiet, I felt compelled to kneel at the side of my bed. With paper and pen in hand, I wrote down my words of communication with The Father, my Christ within. And then the response began to flow, filling me not only with bewilderment, but also with gratitude and peace. I began to make this communication a daily practice. Whatever was in my heart or needed illumination was the focal point for that day's communication.

This Diary of Answered Prayers was so sacred, precious, and personal that I kept these writings hidden, even from my husband. Then one day, Richard found my writings and asked if he could read them. I reluctantly gave him permission. To my amazement, he became very excited and encouraged me to "come out of the closet" and share God's words with the world. I consented although I felt like I was baring my soul to everyone who read these very private words.

It was soon revealed to me that these writings are no more mine than the multiplication tables are mine, so these writings should be shared with all who are seeking Truth. I have no idea why Spirit chose me as one of His channels, but I am eternally grateful for this honor.

I am convinced that all of us have the ability to communicate with God. Some of the keys to effective communication with Spirit are to be relaxed (peaceful), to breathe deeply and remain open for spirit's message.

The answers to our prayers can come to us in many different ways. Answers may come through inspired dictation, as they do with me, through our intuition, "coincidental happenings," a comment from a friend or, through dreams or visions. Regardless of how we receive our answers, the key to effective communication with Spirit is to remain open and honor the messages we are sent.

In God's responses to my prayers, He makes repeated reference to living The Principle if we are to experience The Kingdom of God on earth. The Principle is simply our knowing that we are One with God. God is not outside of us. God is within each and every one of His children. We are One with God. The Principle is our knowing and our acceptance that everything in our life is in divine order, and we are not having these experiences alone. God is with us every step of the way.

The Principle requires us to Let Go and Let God do the work. We are asked to turn our concerns over to Spirit. I have found that being at peace with the world around me is the key to my staying in The Principle.

In my transcription of God's messages, I have avoided rephrasing or altering God's words to make them more readable. You are reading God's words exactly as they were given to me. The only liberties I have taken are my gender inclusive references to God as He/She, and with punctuation and capitalization which you may find unconventional in some instances. I pray you enjoy and grow from God's messages as I have. We welcome your comments and God Bless You.

Billie

He Talks With Me

"A Diary of Answered Prayers" 3-2-77

Dearest Marjorie,

With so very much love
& appreciation over the years.
You will always hold a special
place in my heart. Love

Billie Stevens

Upon awakening one morning, I felt that God had something to say to me. I took paper and a pen from my bedside table and what follows came to me.

I look out upon a world that's new.
The world's not changed, tis just my view
of seeing it aright.

The Oneness of all things I feel.
I know the underlying real
is Life & Love & Light.

I look out upon a world Divine.
It's your world too, not only mine
and all is well.

True Vision helps me clearly see
that God is All Reality
and in Him we dwell.

You are loved

#1 - Tuesday

Oh Divine Christ of Me:

My ever present guide, who knows all Truths, who is my Reality. I come to commune and receive Your communication that will again put me in tune with All good, with All perfection, with wholeness, joy, harmony, with unchanging Reality itself. For the time, I am putting aside all books and relying on You alone. My soul cries out for light. I seem to have been in darkness... weak, struggling, unhappy. Please erase all that is unlike You. Enter into my realization so clearly that nothing else will blot out Your wonderful presence. I need You. I want to be allied with You. I want my spiritual eyes opened to Your abiding Truth. I have had enough of all else for all time. I open my consciousness to Your guidance and teaching. Speak, Lord of my Being. Your servant awaits Your words.

Dearly Beloved Child:

The Truth is simple, of childlike simplicity. Don't complicate Its beauty. I have chosen you, as I have chosen each of my children, to exemplify that trials are like bubbles that burst into nothingness. Much of the time you have lived according to this Principle. Do not get too upset when you fall by the wayside.

It helps you to understand how lost others can seem to be. You are a light, One with God light. Let It shine! There can be no darkness in light. Do not let yourself be hypnotized by anything that is not of God. God... Good... alone, is. When you are feeling joy, harmony, peace, love, perfection, you are wide awake and I AM The Christ living through you, and how I love that. Don't shut me out by feeling opposites (worry, fear, anxiety, hate).

Relax, take it easy! Know that all in the present scene eventually passes away. Do not cling to it. Let it go! Cling only to Me, your very own Christ. Feel that your life is from above. You are held to Me as if by a magic golden thread. Feel raised, lifted up, tall; not existing from the earth, where there seems to be gravity pulling downward! My child, I love You. I know how sincerely you have tried and are trying.

Let Me be your All. Let My light shine upon you and dissipate all errors. Believe that I AM. And then what has seemed material, with disturbances, will be transmuted. You will transcend all so-called blocks and barriers of materiality. Now you will know that your Real and eternal body is spiritual, not unlike the body of God. There is a melting into Oneness. You are cleansed of all impurities. You are whole, complete, perfect, since

Spirit (God) is whole, complete, perfect. Exult in this guidance. Feel the upsurge away from multiplicity and errors.

I am trying to awaken you to your true heritage! Dwell with Me as One. I am glad that you hear Me. I am here to save you and free you from all that is unlike God. I have helped you before in many ways. Please believe that I AM the author, the Source of your salvation. I have guided you, solved problems for you, given you peace and understanding. I am rescuing you now and will lift you to higher heights, clearer vision than you have ever realized before. You are just passing through this valley of shadows.

Do not linger longer in these unwholesome depths. Accept My invitation to raise you; to awaken you from mortal dreaming; to flood you with the joys of the Kingdom, unspeakable. I will never leave you. Never forget Me. I wait patiently for opportunities such as this. I want to renew you, to regenerate you, to restore you to your rightful Beingness. I penetrate every avenue of your consciousness. Truly there is only Me. Do not dilute My purity with half-Truths or mortal lies, I want to be All of you. My love and blessing.

Amen.

#2 - Thursday

Dear Divine Presence and Guide, The Real of Me:

What joy it is to feel Your presence. I love You with such a holy, pure affection. Continue to speak to me, not too softly or gently, so that I can receive every idea. I come to

You with rejoicing and thanksgiving and also to have more needs fulfilled. There are little pieces, like in a jigsaw puzzle, that I need your help in putting together correctly. These pieces are many, but no doubt each one is needed to fit together to form the perfect picture. And now I surrender all these pieces of concern. I have let go of them and have given them to You. So now I am receptive, loving and joyful.

My deep gratitude.

Dearly Beloved Child:

How true that you cannot give over something and still hold onto it. Complete release is necessary. However, in My care, I shall purify, adjust, readjust, and return, not the individual pieces, but the completed solving of this puzzle and the perfect picture.

I am glad you have faith in Me. I will transcend all seeming difficulties, and as a result, you will be enriched, overjoyed and blessed. This is not a stumbling block, but a tremendous opportunity to grow, unfold, and to realize Me ever more near, constantly. I will bring about the perfect answer. Dear child, just stand aside, and with glee in your eyes and a smile on your lips, await My returning gift to you.

Let the beauties, the wonders, the perfection, the joys of the Kingdom unfold. With perfect trust in Me, you will entertain no fears, doubts nor worries. You will grow immeasurably. I exult in this opportunity to live through you and to express, for your happiness is My happiness and vice versa.

You have cleansed the channel so there is no

clogging where darkness impedes. There is only light to lighten your way. Not only to brighten, but to lift your so-called load and to unburden you. Be constant in this attitude. Feel at peace and let your cup run over with "Spiritual Waters" so that others can be refreshed and cleansed.

Oh Dear Christ of Me:

I am so grateful for Your presence and guidance. Please be me. I surrender all that is unlike You. I want You with all my heart to be my livingness. I will endeavor to live life simply. No longer will I let things in the outer disturb me or darken my path. I want no more to stumble because of this darkness. I have had enough of such ignorance.

I start a new chapter, the best I have ever known, because I AM free. I AM whole, I AM light, I AM undisturbed, I AM strong.

On my knees I have sought You, now I will arise. With head in heaven I will keep close to You, One without separation. I have nothing to fear, for You are with me. I am grateful, so very grateful. I have been reborn, the second birth, into Spirit. I AM a new individuality, but never alone, nevermore lost, bewildered! I have been hungry and You have fed me with the fruits of the Spirit. I have been thirsting and You have quenched my desire for all that is unlike You. I have been worried and upset and You have proved, like 2 x 2 always equals 4, that You are my light, in which there is no darkness. I have come to You and I have been filled... filled with the glory of Your perfect Self ! If I sinned, all are cleansed. If I have wronged anyone, I have been forgiven. If I have not seen through the outer into the One essence of Being, I am given another chance. Oh, how I desire to cooperate! Oh, how I wish to be released from all that is not 2 x 2 = 4. Please take over for me. Be me, live through this channel of my individuality and pour out Your blessings upon all whom I encounter.

Glory to God and to my God Self.

#3 - Friday

And now communion time with my wonderful God and my spiritual Christ Self... One with the God Reality:

How wonderful to have rapport with the One. The channel is open for Him to talk with me, to guide, to illumine, to make me whole. Most of all, I am so very thankful for this communication. The guidance that has come through during my life has been beyond words to express. My desire is to continue always in this divine rapport and feel His peace, love, wisdom, joy, guidance and trust.

My great gratitude and love.

Dear Child:

You know water flows freely when a channel is opened to it. And so you have been preparing a channel to let God's presence and power flow into your Beingness and will continue to flow as you feel relaxed, free and flowing on Its current. Then all is easy, beautiful, perfect and joyous as you follow this wonderful Principle of letting go and letting God flow into your Beingness to be the stream of living waters. And so all is well... body, mind and soul. Be at peace and rejoice.

#4 - Saturday

Dear Inner Guide and Joy:

With nothing special in mind, I come to You, just for the ecstasy of feeling our Oneness. I do not want to fall away from the remembrance and practice of such communications. I listen. Speak to me.

My love and gratitude.

Dearly Beloved Child:

How beautiful that you do not come to Me asking for something, but just for the sheer delight of togetherness. You are in tune with Me, otherwise you would not feel so lighthearted, and that your work is so light, too, although accomplishing much.

You and your husband have taken a big step forward in giving the green light to your travel plans. I will be in the midst when decisions are made. I will go ahead to prepare a place for you no matter where your travels take you. Depend on Me. Rely on Me, moment by moment and day by day.

#5 - Sunday

Again Communication, Dear Divine Presence:

What a wonderful realization! Please know that I felt Your loving, healing presence encircling me during the night, giving me the assurance that all is well. You are the substance of this so-called body. You are "nearer than breathing and closer than hands and feet." You are my health, my happiness, my joy, my inspiration.

I am thankful for this perfect blend with You. Please express through me freely. I invite Your wisdom, Your guidance, Your Being. Be me! Shine through me into infinity! Wash away all that seems to be unlike You. Cleanse me from all impurities and darkness. I want more and more vehemently to understand, to cultivate Your awareness and joy.

Thank you.

Dearly Beloved One:
I AM your wholeness, your happiness, your life! I fulfill all your needs according to divine dictates. I AM infinite; All light; All perfection; All glory, and you are One with this Reality. How wonderful that you are aware of this Truth. How easy life can be when you let me carry your so-called burdens, give you ideas and make your decisions. I need you to express through, as you need Me for what is to be expressed.

My love and blessings, Amen.

#6 - Tuesday

Dearest Divine Partner:
How I cherish this time together and I feel You are coming through more clearly as I open up to You more constantly. Throughout the day I try to feel Your abiding presence, and the more this is realized, the more beautifully, perfectly, and easily the day unfolds. So now, once again, I most earnestly invite, most intently listen, and devotedly follow through.

Dearly Beloved Child:

I know I am loved by you. I know your sincerity. I want you to realize that the perfect pattern of livingness in which there is no error, is yours. This One activity which is perfection Itself is your Beingness and the Beingness of all who desire It and claim It.

When one is trying to solve a puzzle, there are challenges, anxieties, frustrations, until the solution is comprehended. Then, it is so simple and so easy. It almost falls into place without effort. And so it is with solving the Divine Puzzle which truly is no longer a puzzle once the solution is seen.

I AM your Puzzle Solver making your way easy, perfect and joyous. I love to be active in your consciousness. I love to be wanted, needed, appreciated. I feel you have opened wide the door for Me to enter and come in. And so minute by minute, day by day, I AM at your side; at your beck and call; eager to fulfill all your needs.

I AM that which always was and never changes. I AM that Reality of you which is the Real you. I AM One with Jesus Christ. One with all the Illumined Souls. All One in God. I welcome you to this Host of Over Souls who love you sincerely and are grateful to have a channel of expression such as you. We are in rapport and it is glorious.

These Masters delight in your request to have Them master and guide your life so that only Godlike qualities manifest in the "outer" as they are in the "inner." As in Heaven, so on earth.

When you are totally in tune and feel this One-ness, you will be unaware of your so-called body. So completely shall it be absorbed into spirituality. So

Problems are for solving... to strengthen your appreciation of The Principle. I AM your "Puzzle Solver"... making your way easy, perfect, and joyous.

perfect will it be in activity and substance, that truly it will be in the Temple of The Living God. There are dimensions of expression even higher. When you are worthy and ready, you will be graduated into higher realizations; ever farther away from the darkness and discords of so-called materiality. You will realize more blessedness, more joy, more ease of living.

Amen.

#7 - Thursday

Dear Wonderful Reality:

How great You are and how wonderful is my I AM Christ. My Real eternity is when I find It and live One with It, seeing all else as passing appearances. I know how joyous, whole and energetic I am when abiding in this dimension; identifying with my true, Real, eternal, spiritual Self . This is my prayer; my goal; my aspiration to always be this One in the inner, but not in its ephemeral atmosphere. From sense to soul is my aspiration while my feet still tread earthly sod.

My love and gratitude.

Dearly Beloved Child:

Keep on trying even when you feel misplaced or out of tune or not in rhythm with your own wonderful Self. It is seeking you as you are trying to find It. To be sure, It is the greatest gift possible. Your own Christ eternal; from the beginning helping you to always arrive and be this One made in the image of God, The Christ.

Your "grades" shall go up as you achieve this realization. But you must first see through the nothingness of earthly materialism. Know that only God essence and presence is Real. Do not be fooled!!

Amen.

#8 - Friday

Dearly Beloved Presence:

How I look forward to this time together each day. With Your help, I feel that I am all set for the day's so-called problems, activities, etc., because I know You are always with me and working all things together for my good and the good of all concerned. And now I listen gratefully, expectantly, joyously... as a little child.

Dearly Beloved One:

I AM a more Real presence than anything that your eyes, ears, all of your so-called physical senses are aware of. I AM unchanging perfection and wisdom; not only Principle but also your loving partner. I want to show you the way so as to avoid pitfalls and unhappiness; to make your life easy and joyous; running over with all of God's blessings.

I want your consciousness to be free from any undue concern about physical well being. You will pass this test if you keep Me in the center of your life. Keep alive in your awareness what you really are the perfect creative idea of what is behind the "out picturing" of man in the outer. This is the blueprint for each and every human expression, and in every minutest aspect there is

perfection, wisdom and harmony.

Do not deal with effects. Go back to this perfect pattern which is cause, and feel that this is the Real you. This is your true inheritance, the Son, God's perfect gift to you. But you must go beyond the outer wrappings (the visible) and accept the gift within. Then you will realize your Oneness with God and know that all that the Father has is thine. This is the link that connects, like plugging an electrical appliance into the outlet to connect with supply. God's supply is infinite.

When you accept this Whole Truth in its entirety, you will feel whole, healthy, complete, perfect, happy, at ease, poised, balanced. Then God works through you to complete your every task; to guide your decisions and activities; to live through you.

Do not mistake the visible world for Reality; it is only effect, passing, ephemeral, here today and gone tomorrow. Put no other gods (illusive beliefs) before Me. The way is easy, not difficult. Do not make it difficult by applying erroneous beliefs.

I show you the way, but you must walk in it. You must apply the Truth Principles yourself; daily, hour by hour, minute by minute. You are turning the snags into pearls and you are being blessed and helped by the Heavenly Hosts until you fully awaken as one of them. They are helping you. Believe.

Love and blessings, Amen.

Dear God:

I would be strong, firm, true to Your teachings. I know You are All. The desire of my heart is to keep centered in You. I would be whole... wholly Thine. I accept! I believe! I thirst for this teaching even more!

#9 - Saturday

Dearly Beloved Presence:

Again our communion. I need more and more to feel Your presence, guidance and help. I pray that I will keep more alert to that which needs to be done... "on earth as it is in Heaven." With Your help, that shall be accomplished.

Yesterday, after affirming that I would not allow things in the outer to upset me, and divert me from my Center of Peace, I was tested... much like in mathematics classes... to solve the problem calmly, but the result may not be in accordance with Your Truth. By oversight, we (my husband and I) have let our passports expire and this was not discovered until yesterday noon. There seemed to be a dark cloud hiding Your light. There was fear, worry from the American Automobile Association because of the time element (regarding our departure for South America in a week). Dear divine Christ, help solve this dreamlike illusion. Clear the horizons! Manifest Your perfect will and assurance! Speak!

Dear Child:
Problems are for solving, to strengthen your appreciation of the Principle. You have not failed... and I never fail. Please believe, this too is for good. Keep your attitude positive, healthy, thankful, peaceful. I promise to make all things straight, even the seeming crooked places. I go ahead and prepare the way. You have nothing to fear. Expect good!

Clouds are ephemeral and they come and go, but I abide forever. Right in the midst of this "problem" I AM active, powerful, positive. I AM the Engineer to bring about all good, perfection. Have faith in Me. Relax. Already it is done. I will never leave you or forsake you.

What a glorious feeling, trust. Love and thanksgiving will result when all that I have said is manifest in the outer. You are My beloved Child and you are progressing and unfolding because you are humble, sincere, loving. Do not forsake these attitudes! Be One with Me. Together we know that all is well. I delight in being your guide and helper and I will lift you above all errors.

Love and blessings, Amen.

#10 - Sunday

Dear Wonderful Jesus Christ. My Own I AM Eternal Self:

I really need You this morning. I have fallen off the track and I am out of tune with You. There are manifestations in my outer self that are not normal (Nose, cheek, tummy). Please help me to get in tune with You again so I may once again feel Your peace, joy, perfection, wholeness, purity, goodness. I must once again identify with the Truth of who I AM and not with the third dimension. Take over for me.

Love and gratitude.

Dear Child:
You have not yet awakened this morning from your mortal dreaming. All is well, perfect, joyous in the Realm of Reality, the Kingdom of God where your true Self abides. Relax the outer and let go of concerns, anxieties and worries about anything in the third dimension. Do not speak falsely by saying "I" when you mean your shadowy, illusive body. The "I" of you is The Christ... your true identity, One with God where All is perfection. Awaken. Stay alive in God. God loves you as you are.

#11 - Monday

Dearly Beloved Presence:
I am sure You heard my plea yesterday and when I awakened this morning, there was Your answer... The Truth... to be lived, applied:
This too, shall pass. I see through its dreamlike mirage to the One Reality... to my I AM... in perfect harmony, rhythm, wholeness with God, light, wisdom. There is only The One.
Thank You for this blessing, which already has made my day unfold easily, beautifully, perfectly. By grace I have been saved. I will forever be grateful. I will never forget nor neglect to live this Truth. I love you.

Dearest Child:
One falls asleep and awakens, but the Principle never changes! The Principle is the Realm of Realty that has nothing to do with time or space. It is infinite... eternal. Keep centered... relax, feel free and easy. Rejoice

that All is well.

Amen.

#12 - Tuesday

Dear Eternal I AM Christ:
        Some time ago I felt so uplifted and elated because I had found my eternal, spiritual, Real Self. I knew this was truly my everlasting entity and I let It live out of my center. Such rejoicing for such a find. I wanted to keep and be this One Self forever, but somehow there was a loss in contact and I have been searching ever since. Occasionally there is a glimpse, a brief connection. My prayer is to be returned to this One, Real Self where I AM.

I give thanks and my love.

Dearest Child:
        This is the reason for living. To transcend the mortal world and arrive at the point of your spiritual, perfect Self . This is the answer to all morale problems, anxieties, frustrations. The journey from sense to soul requires much self disciplining and a fervent desire to achieve Oneness with God Reality. You have traveled this "high road" for many years and the yield has been plentiful in peace, wholeness, joy and prosperity, but you cannot stand still. There are more steps to be taken upward and onward. The glimpses indicate you are on the right track. Keep going. The hand of God is reaching out for yours as you extend yours to Him. Know that you are loved.

17

#13 - Thursday

Dearly Beloved Christ Mind... God:

Trying to tune into You has been my earnest desire and I believe the mist is disappearing and I am seeing You and my own true Self more clearly as One. With Your help I am guided and made whole and grateful to You beyond words.

Dear Child:

The clutter in your life, the anxieties, are clearing and so you can see the whole Truth of Reality. And with the clearing you will recognize your own wholeness, peace, harmony, well-being, perfection. You are growing and unfolding. When you reach the mountain top and breathe the pure air of Spirit, you will know the struggle and persistence have been worthwhile. Never forget, it is not easy for others to make the journey from sense to soul, but it is the salvation and the only salvation for each and every one.

My grace has enveloped you whether you are busy or asleep. My grace has made you whole; wholly One with Me. I have chosen you as you have chosen Me. Together it is glorious, wonderful, full of goodness. Keep on keeping on, dear child. You are doing well.

Love and blessings, Amen.

#14 - Friday

Dearly Beloved Reality:

What a joy to come to You for communication

which results in renewal, refreshing vitality, courage, peace, wholeness, the glory of Oneness. I love You and praise Your abiding help. Your hand has guided me in many ways; to find my daughter's letters, to facilitate our passports, to make our schedules, to put all things in divine order. I know You will ever be near me and I will keep in rapport with You regardless of time and space, which to You are nothing. Speak to me. I listen.

Dear Child of Mine:

I feel so close to you and I am grateful to you as a channel through which I can speak words of Truth. Please believe that even though there may not be evidences in the outer, My healing presence is always pulsating in perfect rhythm, light, balance, harmony. Always behold Me as you see through the mask worn by materiality. The price paid for glory, abiding as One with Me in "the Secret Place of the Most High," is to put no other gods before Me. Know that I AM All there truly is. All seeming else is untrue, ephemeral, a lie. Are you willing to pay this price which will unfold treasures of infinite worth and grandeur, of glories that the mortal man could never experience? This Principle is true no matter where you are. It is changeless and always in operation. My joy is your joy and vice versa. My wholeness is your wholeness. My perfection is your perfection. There is only the One, without separation, exception or variation.

You have been going through your divine initiation which now is a new beginning. You have been reborn. You have shed the outer shell of the third or human (mortal) dimension. You no longer need it. When

the bird breaks through its shell, it casts it aside because it no longer needs it. This act of initiation is the beginning of a new dimension. That of being Spirit and abiding in Spirit. You will fly as the bird; unweighted and free.

Your soul will take wings and not be pulled downward. You will feel light and be light. A song will sing in your heart and all will be melodious and in tune. You will know that this Real you is The Christ. Through the power and the love and the glory of Jesus Christ and all the Heavenly Hosts who have been helping you. You have ascended. There is no regressing. You can never, and would never want to, return to the third dimension, mortal living; no more than a bird could return to being in its shell.

I love to teach you, dear child. I love to see you graduated from sense to soul... to live easily, joyously and perfectly while still manifesting on the earth plane... in the world but not of it. Congratulations to you.

Dear Wonderful Presence:
Humbly, I thank you. I AM Yours forever!

#15 - Saturday

Dearest Father, Mother God. My own Divine Instructor, Guide and Friend who is closer than breathing:
How I love You and thank You for the Truth You have unveiled to me. Oh, may I keep It in my heart and follow It as we start on our two week journey to South America. May these Truths ever loom bright and glorious in my consciousness wherever I may be; releasing me from all

anxieties, worries and the bondage of mortality. Speak to me with the most important guidance to maintain throughout these days and always.

Thanks be to you.

Dear One:

You are perfect now. You coincide with me and I AM perfection. Forget all else. Abide in Reality. Truth reigns. My mind is your mind. I will instruct more and more as you proceed. Only believe God is All. All else is seeming... a myth... a mirage. Be wise! Be free! Be loving! Be whole! Be Me!

My love and blessings, Amen.

#16 - Monday

Dear Divine Presence and Guide:

. It has been quite a while since being down on my knees communing with You, but I have felt Your wonderful presence with me during our long trip of many, many thousands of miles and I have tried to practice the Truth Principles You have so lovingly given to me. Through Your grace and love I have felt well, strong, happy, harmonious throughout these two busy weeks in South America. All our needs were fulfilled and our experience has been fruitful. I have not forgotten You nor Your loving help as a result of my contact with You and my earnest, sincere pleas for being lifted out of third dimension conflicts, mortal seemings, temporal adversities, etc., into the pure, ecstatic Realm of Your eternal Kingdom.

You know how grateful I am and as I adjust to normal living again and have many duties, decisions, etc., may I ever receive Your guidance. And throughout the new challenges to come, (out of town family visits, baby sitting, entertaining, etc.), may all these be opportunities to come closer to You so that I may feel Your Oneness with All, and partake of Your wholeness, happiness, and well-being.

With so very much gratitude and love.

Dearly Beloved Child:
I have never left you. When you needed Me, I was there. When you had times of experiencing awe inspiring scenes, behold, I was there, as I AM with you now. What joy to express through you!

As you climb mountains, as you have been doing, you become stronger. This conditioning prepares you for more climbs and higher ascents. Live one moment at a time, receiving My guidance, inspiration and help. You will see that all will fall into place easily, perfectly, gloriously because you have given Me the authority to take over. Effortlessly, all will thus be accomplished. You will be renewed, restored, revitalized, moment by moment and day by day as you abide in the present Reality.

Never feel that you are doing anything alone, for I AM the power, the wisdom, the love! All of God and His Heavenly Hosts are aware of you and your desire to live fully, completely, wholly. And there is nothing beside this unchanging Reality.

Stay with Principle, with Truth and all else will be observed as eventually passing away. Be a "seer" and

see through mirage. Be wise and know that your I AM is One with God, in perfect harmony and Oneness. I love you as you so genuinely love Me. It is a wonderful relationship. So be it.

#17 - Tuesday

Dearest Christ Reality, My Very Own, "I AM:"
How wonderful to feel Your holy (whole) presence and to know You hear me always and answer my prayers. Such rapport is the height of livingness. Speak to me, showing me how I can better keep in harmony with You consistently and constantly. For this is the glory, the joy, the unspeakable blessing.

My love and gratitude.

Dearly Beloved Child:
It is to the Real of you, your I AM that I speak... Spirit to Spirit, Reality to Reality, yet All One. Already the "I AM" is and always has been and always will be in step with Me. Remember the sermon message that came through to you several years ago, Keep Step. In this simple, childlike allegory was given the complete Principle of Life.
There is a divine harmony, tempo, activity in God's Kingdom, (on earth as in Heaven) that flows along in a certain rhythm, much like a current in a beautiful peaceful stream. If you can feel, be aware of this rhythmic flow, and let your entire Being (body, mind, soul) be merged into Oneness with this, so there is no separation, you will find yourself living in the Kingdom of Heaven

right here and now. Automatically, All of God becomes All of you... harmony will be felt, questions, problems, perplexities will be solved, joy will permeate your Being. To be in perfect step, in rhythm with the divine, is the answer.

Know that you are loved and are safe in the "Everlasting Arms" of God.

But to go against the current, in the limited capacity of the little separate self, is not only inviting hardships, troubles, hurts, and dissatisfaction, but also can be fatal. The activity that was meant for good, to help you, when you keep step with It, can be the very force for destruction when not applied according to God's way, as Jesus taught.

This is Principle, divine activity, never deviating, never changing, always the same. To let go and let God is the essence of this lesson. Feel your Self floating joyously, easily, perfectly on the divine current and know that underneath are the Everlasting Arms.

Remember when you applied this consciously, constantly, fervently, joyously many years ago, how your back problem was completely dissipated. But so often one has to be reminded of this Principle. Do not forget God; He never forgets you. The divine current flows on and on, whether you place yourself, your hopes, your convictions, your faith, and trust in It or not. Be wise. Live One with God and rejoice!

#18 - Wednesday

Dear Wonderful God Reality. The One Divine Essence:

I am seeing through all in the outer, letting go of my hold on things, persons, places. I have become One with You, and this day, as yesterday, unfolds easily, perfectly, happily and yet I am accomplishing much. I thank You and love You and I know that I have a part to play; a discipline to adhere to in order to break through the block of the third dimension and let Your wonderful Self come through.

This Principle can be applied at all times in all

places. How grateful I am to have reached a plateau where I can see through the sham to the One, great I AM.

My greatest love to You.

Dear Child:
Few answer the call although all have the same privilege as you. The Divine Call is an inner urge; the activity of The Christ within, to seek further and further, much as a seed in the ground pushes up to come into the light. Only forgetfulness, indifference and lack of faith can prevent the upward and onward unfolding into the Oneness of God Being. Never accept the appearances in the material world to be God Reality. Destroy, dematerialize, look through their so-called reality. By God's grace, you have seen the light.

You are loved.

#19 - Thursday

Dearest Divine Reality. Christ of Me:
This is the most anticipated time of my day. I ask You for direction, guidance and help; and always there is response. I have beseeched You and You have heard. I have praised Your wonderful Self and You have reminded me that I AM made in Your image. So it is with great gratitude that I thank You for my wholeness. You have given me strength, confidence and joy. I dwell upon each precept that unfolds from You to me. Speak. Your servant hears You.

Dearly Beloved Child:

The way of Christ is not easy. The way is narrow and straight, but once you put your feet upon It, It is much like an escalator which carries you along by its own power. To be sure, there are times when it seems necessary to have interruptions. But always go back and get back on the escalator and you will reach the heights effortlessly. (Do this whenever you are interrupted in your meditations with Me.)

You need not do the climbing yourself when you have reached this dimension. Just relax and enjoy the ride. Beauty abounds everywhere. It is I coming into manifestation. The earth is awakening from its long winter's sleep. And so you too have awakened. The drowsy stupor is disappearing. The mists are seen for what they are; vapors of nothingness, mirages that would cause unhappiness and suffering if, in your ignorance, you allowed yourself to be deluded, hypnotized, mesmerized.

Jesus Christ saw the Truth and Reality of the everlasting Kingdom and He is your helper, keeper and guide. The Truth is simple and easy when your consciousness is devoid of opposites (of God) and is uncluttered with the shadows of third dimension materiality. Keep simple. Keep pure, even as a little child. Refrain from criticism, condemnation, worry, fear, anxiety. Be unselfed.

Think not of glamorizing the personal self and of expounding this personal self, for it is nothing and will only confuse and upset. My glory is your glory. My Kingdom is yours, although you have just begun to be aware of It, and only now to have the courage to enter It.

Heavenly Hosts are welcoming you to dwell (while still manifesting on earth) in Its midst, and be One with the All.

Discipline the little self constantly. Look through the sham to where I AM and you are. Here there is no friction, no sorrow, no discouragement for all is well and all eternity is God. Keep awake. Slumber not in mortal dreaming. I AM with you. Feel My presence, My love, My guidance, My support.

With infinite love, Amen.

#20 - Friday

Dearest Father-Mother-Teacher:

There were so many interferences this morning. The time for our communication is later than usual, but ever so sincere and fervent. How easy it is to let clutter in the outer invade; and how difficult at times to clear my little mind and remember where I put things.

Dear Father-Mother, take me under Your wings. Dissipate all the shadows. Make Your precepts so clear to me that I dwell and abide in Principle and in Your love.

Thank you, fervently.

Dear Child:

Don't struggle! Just let go! Nothing is so important that you should allow it to cast shadows. Nothing is a no-thing, a big bubble of seeming importance, but doomed to be punctured and to be no more. But My Kingdom endures forever. Here is where your so-called

problems are solved; where peace, poise and ease are regained. Let nothing interfere with your realization of The Christ, which is your true Self. I will always be with you.

Infinite love and blessings, Amen.

#21 - Saturday

Dear Father-Mother-Friend and Divine Helper:
     Time has been busy. But I am so thankful that all is well and all is unfolding according to Your perfect plan. We picked up our daughter, her husband and children at the airport this a.m.; served lunch, and now it is "siesta" time for our grandchildren. I know I will need Your sustaining help, wisdom and guidance during the coming week. Already I thank You that "it is done." You and I, we can do all things. I rest in peace, hope, joy and thanksgiving.

Dear Beloved Child:
     You are well cared for and My help will extend to all your loved ones. They will see you in a new light... as a child of light and love. I desire to express through you. Be My expression! Whatever is for the good of each and all will unfold. Keep close to Me in thought and deed so that there is contact and Oneness. All is well in the perfect Kingdom. Recognize Reality and give no recognition to what is not Reality.
     Live only in the present moment, looking not back in regret or worry; nor ahead with anxiety or concern. Right now I AM "all right." I will be with you. I AM with you to share all the glory and joy of your family.

29

#22 - Sunday

Dear Father-Mother-Helper-Friend:

It is with Your help that I am sustained, soothed, given strength and encouragement during this "testing time." Endurance prevails when I abide close to You. Help me to keep Your attributes of joy, peace, contentment, well-being ever alive and active. Give me wisdom to know what to say and what to do. Live through me. This is my plea.

With infinite love and gratitude.

Dearly Beloved Child:

I am observing you and am aware of your good attitude. I have faith in you to come out on top. No burden or responsibility is great when I carry the load. Believe this! Put your "load" on Me. Feel light, free, unfettered!

In order to ascend completely, all aspects of humanity must be met with and overcome. If you fall, pick yourself up immediately and go on. Have no regrets nor anxieties. I see you as an overcomer. Jesus, The Christ said, "I have overcome the world." Be of the same attitude as your big brother. Be attitude! Be joy! Be wholeness! Be peace! You must now prove what you have accepted with the intellect. You have the formula which always produces the right answer. By My grace and My love, you have been anointed and illumined.

Amen.

#23 - Tuesday

Dearest Father-Mother-The Christ:
It is to You that I look for strength, vitality, patience, love, well-being. Please fulfill me in every way. I feel Your sustaining grace and soothing affection. Teach me more as I progress up the mountain. I need You as You need me for Your expression.

With very much gratitude.

Dearest Child:
Strength comes from use. Unfoldment and more enlightenment result from practicing the Truth Principles I have given you. Apply these and grow! Unfold! And ever and ever become more My likeness! I love you and rejoice in your progress.

#24 - Wednesday

Dearest Divine Christ, Angel of My Being:
I hope I haven't disappointed You by not being quiet and giving heed to Your wonderful guidance and help. I have needed You, but perhaps have not been receptive enough because of outer activities with the visit of Joan, Barclay and the grandchildren. I feel tired because I have not kept our avenue of communication open. Forgive me for my omissions, and give me an ever fresh supply of inspiration, strength, well-being, peace and guidance. I AM Your Prodigal. Give me Your assurance and help.

With love and gratitude.

Dearly Beloved Prodigal:
When everything does not seem to be in harmony with My perfect Kingdom, it should be a symbol that you have wandered off in consciousness from your divine home where you rightfully belong.

I have been with you. I have strengthened and redeemed you from negative influences. I AM your center, your guide, your Source of All good. I am pleased with your sincere and ardent efforts. Just keep on keeping on. Look at the positive, the cheery, the constructive. Let go of personal innuendos, desires, influences. Keep close to Me and keep aware of My unfailing presence. Light reveals the way; darkness causes stumbling. Take it easy. Feel light and buoyant. Be a good exponent of Truth, but do not preach. Guard against being annoyed and keep cheery. You are passing your test. Keep it up! Strength will flow to you beyond comprehension, as well as My love and blessings.

Amen.

#25 - Thursday

Dearest Father-Mother God:
It is You I need so very much for strength, endurance, patience, wisdom. Help me through this testing time. Let me feel Your well-being and guiding hand. Sustain me, soothe me, help me. I love You.

Thanks be to You.

Dear Struggling Child:
Tests often seem very difficult, but no more difficult than you are capable of handling. You will come up with the right answers because you have started with the right premise. God Alone Is... and Is All. All else eventually fades away.

Be a seer and see through the shadows! Relax when you can and feel that under all are the Everlasting Arms. Always, I AM with you to sustain, help, guide, fulfill. Believe this.

#26 - Friday

Dearest Father-Mother-Guide:
Communion time! How I need You to give me balance, peace, poise, a feeling that all is well, because You are All. Speak to me encouraging words of strength, patience and renewal.

Dearly Beloved Disciple:
You are trying to discipline your words, actions, thoughts, feelings, etc. I AM with you to strengthen your efforts. Steel is made strong because of strain. You are being made true as steel because you have risen above material's downward pull. Feel the upward pull more and more; away from the gravity of the earth. Transcend this dimension. You are graduating to a higher dimension. I AM ever with you. It is I who is lifting your burdens, bringing joy out of seeming darkness, buoyancy out of strain.

You have been letting Me put together the jig saw puzzle and you are doing better at keeping your personal

self subordinated. **You have been a faithful and sincere student, tried and true, and I am pleased. But never give up trying to improve and become more Christ-like. That goal is the greatest and most worthy to make efforts to achieve. It is much a quality of letting... and letting go... letting Me take over... letting go the personal... two in the field. One must let go in order to achieve Heaven on earth. Keep close to Me.**

My Love and blessings, Amen.

#27 - Saturday

Dearest Christ Within, My Father-Mother God:
    Communion is a sweet privilege. To You I can confess my weaknesses and seek Your help to overcome them. One of these weaknesses is talking before organizing my thoughts; speaking so carelessly, thoughtlessly, lightly. I speak words that do not express my true ideas. Help me to speak wisely. Help me to lessen my overflowing talk. Help me to be more poised, relaxed, wise. May my speech be brief, to the point and meaningful. Help me to feel Your strength, well-being and perfection. So often this week I have wandered away from Your central Reality. Perhaps I have not passed this "test" as You would have me. Forgive me for my shortcomings. Make me more like You. Show me the way.

My thanks.

Dearly Beloved Child:
    It is the motive behind words that is important,

not the words. Being centered in God, as you have so
tried, should result in right expression. Do not be too
critical with yourself, but try to talk less. Give fewer
orders and let go of outer concern. Let others choose
their own paths, even if they make mistakes. You are not
responsible for their choices. By their hurts, they will
gain wisdom. Let go all concern. Your only concern
should be to practice the Principles I have so lovingly
given you.

Get in tune with Reality. When you are not
feeling joy, strength, fullness of life; you are out of
harmony with Me (Reality). Be "care-less" in the sense
that you care less for things, effects, etc. in the outer. Be
carefree... give less concern to what others say, think, do
"What is that to you; follow you Me." Being care-less
about responsibilities, tasks, is opening the door to a
freer, more enjoyable Christ way of life.

Be care-less; Christ-more. You are learning. Be
good to yourself by letting go all the anxieties, cares,
concerns of the little self. Keep on trying... Keep on
keeping on. I am always with you. I care for your Christ
well-being to express as you.

Amen.

#28 - Sunday

Dear Father-Mother-Helper-Guide and Teacher:
It is by means of Your presence, Your help, Your
assurance and guidance that I have been able to take on the
extra load and make it to the summit. And because you have
expressed through me, I feel no great weariness or fatigue.

Nor do I have regrets or headaches. If I have adequately passed this test, it is because of Your help. It is my prayer that I have grown in illumination; in understanding of Your Principles; in compassion, tolerance and poise. I have so much (in the way of negatives) to overcome. But I am criticizing less, letting go more. Continue to teach me.

Thank you.

Dear Child:

The past week should give you confidence that endurance is equal to need. As long as you keep in touch with Me; the All Good, Reality, The Christ, you have nothing to fear! Only when you stray away from The Christ Center do you feel alone, weak, incapable. If you continue to feel that I have carried your load, you will have no weakness. Continue to let your heart overflow with gratitude that all falls into its proper place easily, perfectly, harmoniously; and that all is well.

Continue to dwell in present time. I AM right now; perfect, whole, complete. I AM is my eternal name and heritage. Please know that I go before you to prepare the way. To make the rough places smooth, to fulfill all needs. You have expressed much love, patience and good will. I am pleased with your efforts, but know that more constant, Godlike qualities will unfold. Keep on. Know that you need not worry about tomorrow when you trust in Me. I AM infinite and abundance is your heritage... abundance of All Good. My love and blessings are upon you. By grace, you have been saved.

Amen.

#29 - Monday

My great love to Jesus Christ. My God. My unchanging Reality:

   I have always felt Your Reality, but my search has been how to find and align with It. Sometimes It is all very clear to me and then I reach a higher plateau. It is a constant unfoldment as long as I keep One with the Principle given me. Then I feel so gloriously thankful, joyous and whole. My goal; my supreme achievement in life is to find God. The Truth and Reality.

My love and great appreciation.

Dear Child:

   No goal could possibly be more fulfilling. It is beyond riches, popularity, fame. Keep One with God and let God solve all your so-called problems. Let God show the way and give you the answers while you relax on His Everlasting Arms. Be at ease and relax on the divine current and your life will be easy, whole, beautiful and filled to overflowing with all of God's blessings. You have sought and you have found. The Heavenly gates have been opened. All is well.

Praise God.

#30 - Tuesday

Dearest Father-Mother-Teacher:

   Alone with You... what a privilege and solace! Your teachings are Golden Treasures, but I fall away from them so often. Give me insight to steer away from personal down-falls. Too often the little self is focused upon desiring sympathy, pity, glorification. I need Your help to transcend this seeming problem.

Also, teach me to keep Your perfection more constantly in my consciousness. Then I will know the out picturing must be perfect too. You are my guide, my strength, my wisdom, my health, wholeness and well-being. Live through me. I will try to keep open the channel and dwell and abide in Your Kingdom.

Gratefully and lovingly.

Dearly Beloved Child and Student:
I teach you because I love you. My Principles are simple and easy but demand constant vigilance. Do not be swayed by the circumstances, conditions, remarks, opinions in the outer. "What is that to you? Follow you Me." Do not feel swamped with work and activities. All will fall into place perfectly, easily, joyously if you so allow.

Remember always... there is an easy and a difficult way. Choose My way. Let Me lighten your load and lift your burdens. I AM more powerful than you could ever imagine. I AM so very gentle. I will never force or coerce. I AM infinite yet, I am interested in your individual soul, The Christ, for we are One. Choose wise-ly. Feel light, buoyant and happy. All is well.

Take one task at a time; feeling each one is to bless you. In quietude, there is attunement. In gratitude, there is peace. In love, there is perfection. Keep close to Me and feel Me and know I AM your constant guide,

protector, teacher and friend.

#31 - Wednesday

Dear "Angel of My Divine Presence"... Dear Christ of Me:
    You are ever watching over; guiding, helping, instructing. This is our exclusive time again, for which I am grateful. During this period of highest receptivity, kindly pour Yourself out to my waiting consciousness. Please completely annihilate any and all thorns in my side so that I am no longer aware of them or give them even the slightest heeding. Help me to see my True Self as being pure, clean, wholly Thine so no adversary, whether mental or physical, can ever enter in. I surrender my all to Your loving and wise care. Take over. Be me.

My love and gratitude.

Dearly Beloved Child:
    Yes, I AM your Guardian Angel and My every desire for you is one of wholeness, joy, love, completeness, peace, light. When you tune in to Me and are aware of My presence, there is an interplay of divine activity... a Oneness... a perfection of Beingness. Do not ever doubt or forget that I AM your own angel... to guide, teach, help, direct, fulfill. Ask Me what you will that is of My Kingdom, God's Kingdom, that is My All.
    I see you want vitality, youthfulness, beauty of Spirit. Already that is yours because My infinite Kingdom abounds in this essence. Accept! Rejoice! Enjoy. Never feel bottled up or feel that your life is limited to your physical boundaries. That is not so! In Truth, you

39

are as infinite as I AM. But you must awaken to this Reality of you. Let your consciousness expand into its full limitlessness.

Life need not be petty and confined. That is the prison that mortality sentences humanity to. Let go the chains of pity, anxieties, responsibilities, concerns, worry, fear, doubt. They only lock you in. They are no more real than the upsetting dream of last night. When you awakened, these seeming antagonistic monsters were gone. So keep awake to My Kingdom and My ever watchfulness over you; eager to give as you receive. There is nothing besides Me. Believe. Do not live a lie. Ever abide in Truth.

My love for you is infinite, Amen.

#32 - Thursday

Dearest Angel of My Divine Christ:
This is our sacred time together. I always need this daily in-filling of Your perfect essence to make me whole, and to give me Your peace that "passeth all understanding." It seems I falter too often, like a little toddler learning to walk. Help me to fall less often. Give me strength to overcome obstacles, to have patience, compassion and understanding with others. Infuse my consciousness with convictions of Your perfection. Teach me more!

My love and gratitude.

Dearest Toddler:
Your very desire to achieve a realization of per-

fection is half the battle. Push aside from your mental acceptance all that is unlike unto Me, The Christ. Keep dedicated and consecrated to the One Reality. Waver less, toddle less. You already have the built-in strength to overcome; to come up over all seeming error and imperfections; to heights of Christ perfection that annihilate all seeming elseness. Walk tall. Think infinitely. Feel peaceful, poised, relaxed. The elseness is what has been called Satan or the devil. It is a seemingness: errors, untruths, unreal. Do not get mixed up with lies that result in confusion and unhappiness.

Know that to each one you meet, there is an angel observing; trying to guide, instruct, heal. Much as I am proving to you. See no other Reality in others. It takes an angel to greet or salute another angel. Keep on this level. Living then becomes ecstatic, beautiful, worthwhile... on earth as it is in Heaven. This is My desire for you. Let us be One. My grace redeems and makes whole. My love restores.

#33 - Tuesday

Dearest Lover of My Soul:

I greet You and love You as another day begins. This was a very special day for my parents as they took the vow of matrimony 66 years ago and are still together on this earthly plane. It is also a special day for my husband and me for we are planning to attend a baseball game this evening. This will be our first time to the new Riverfront Stadium. How do these things fit into the spiritual pattern... into the Truth of Being? I listen for Your voice and rejoice that You hear me always.

Dearly Beloved Object of My Love:

Although in Truth we are One, your consciousness must evolve to the spiritual level; the level of awareness of your true Being. And so I greet this Reality of you which is Real and intact, even though you have not completely awakened to who you really are. You have the intellect, but that is only the first step. Knowledge must be transcended into the Realm of true Reality where just words are insufficient. It is a state of true Mastership and this is your inheritance. Seek and find as you are. In this true Realm of Reality, time is not a factor. The 66 years of your parent's marriage is as a day. On the mortal scene it is as a picture that moves, passes, disappears.

Likewise, the pleasures of the world (ball games, "firsts," etc.) are as scenes cast on a screen... fleeting, unsubstantial, ephemeral. This does not mean they are not to be participated in and enjoyed. But be wise. Be willing to take them or leave them. Do not put undue importance on these activities; for by so doing, you may be risking drifting away from your Christ Center. Do not forfeit the abiding for the fleeting.

Discipline yourself to abide in consciousness with Me in all ways; always observing the comings and goings of the outer world, but not getting mixed up with involvements. Do not adulterate, for a house divided against itself will fall. In Truth, this is the Principle which, when followed, will bring untold joys... greater than words can reveal. Live normally. Alive, alert, but always abiding in the Reality of the Screen rather than the performances of lights and shadows on it.

#34 - Wednesday

Dearest Divine Guru:
   How I look forward to the time each day when I am alone, when I AM All One with You. Such glorious silence, expectation, peace, communion. I am receptive and open to Your teachings, whatever they may be. I love You deeply and my heart is overflowing with gratitude.

All my love.

Dearly Beloved Student:
   How nicely you are progressing and unfolding into spiritual Truth. Your spiritual eyes have been gradually opening so that the intensely bright light of God's illumination will not startle. You are being conditioned and Truth is being administered to you in small amounts. A rose does not quickly emerge from a bud. There is an unfolding process that is not only beautiful, but also scientific. And nature gives innumerable examples of this process. And so having emerged from the bud dimension, the full bloom of the rose follows.
   And what fragrance, what beauty, what glory! All this is trying to tell something to the receptive heart that is ready to become One with the Principle so as to perceive righteously. And so little by little, as the bud unfolds to become the beautiful rose, so are you being conditioned to receive this glorious awakening to the Truth. No longer will your eyes be blinded by the outpouring of illumination. All the Heavenly Hosts are with you, to support, to observe your new birth into the true Realm of Reality.

How could anyone living in the third dimension of humanhood, where all "things" in the world seem so real and substantial to the senses, accept the Truth that the Father's Real Kingdom transcends all this?! How willing would such a one be to look through his so-called possessions; the materiality of houses, cars, etc., and see the Abiding Substance? For it is necessary first to surrender one's hold on these earthly things so that; unencumbered, and unburdened, but just free and open; he can accept the Heavenly Treasures.

And so, until one has been fully conditioned, and has graduated from kindergarten and the elementary grades, is he qualified to receive the Divine Diploma. Then he knows by the grace of God and by His divine love, that the One Real Kingdom, although invisible to human eyes, can be seen, felt, perceived as One, pervading everywhere. This is a wonderful abiding presence that can be entertained, communicated with... All infinity is open and available!

Ponder this in your heart. It is so very wonderful and glorious. Live in this dimension. You are ready, and never more will you want to fall in consciousness to the lower third dimension of the world where troubles, anxieties, and things of materiality seem so real.

It is like being in a dream state, but your eyes are open wide, and you know the true situation; that you really are awake and can take the attitude, "What is all this 'nonsense' to me? I have arisen and I am following You awake, sure, thankful." These teachings are making it possible and easy to master all conditions in the world. You are in the world, but not of it.

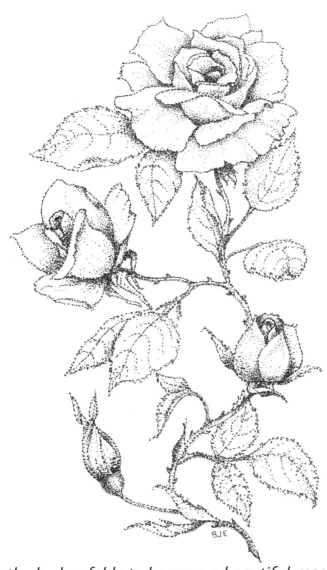

As the bud unfolds to become a beautiful rose, so are you being conditioned to receive this glorious awakening of the Truth.

#35 - Thursday

Dear Wonderful One Reality, One Presence, One Power, One Life, One Substance:

All One, equally present everywhere. In wisdom I must identify the presence of my life, my body, my All, to be identical and One with the Oneness and Allness of God Reality. How then could there be any imperfection, aging... since God never changes and is All perfection, glory, wholeness? This requires much illumination, dedication, humility! In wisdom, to see through the sham, and shadow of the passing outer panorama, scene and behold the One God in whom I dwell and have my Being. This should be and could be very simple, but much pre-crossing out, giving up, wiping out, must take place. The annihilation of all but God. And then, only God (with my I AM) will reign supreme. This is the Truth, and I pray to my God to receive me as His own while still a shadow here on earth.

My love and praise.

My Dear Child:
   Come unto Me, in wisdom, freedom, joy, exhilaration! Having accepted the One God, the One Reality to be All-in-All, you have released your concern about shadows, the comings and goings of fictitious man and his whereabouts. Be about your Father's business and be at peace. Rejoice that after searching, climbing, seeking, persevering, you have found God and your One and only Self ... the One Reality.

Amen.

#36 - Friday

Dearest Divine Co-Partner:
You are my abiding and never failing partner...
always have been and always will be... whether recognized
or not. I love You and thank You for Your wonderful
presence. I am grateful for the many eternal Truths You have
revealed to me, which just makes me eager and hungry for
even more.

Gratefully and lovingly.

Dearly Beloved Child, My Eternal Partner:
The avenue or channel through which I am
revealing becomes even more open as it is used. In Truth,
All of Me is All of You, which, remember, was a title to a
message that came through to you and was later pub-
lished. There is no separation or limitation. The seeming
blocks or separation are caused by ignorance; not know-
ing the Truth of Being, or negligence to keep in rapport,
or immersing the little self in worries, doubts, fears,
hates, anxieties. But My Kingdom is peace, love, har-
mony, joy. Choose to abide therein; to awaken to the
Truth that, already, in Reality, you are abiding in this
divine abode.
Do not try to attain peace, joy, love from the
earth, from humankind; for these are not lasting, nor
genuine. They are as fleeting as the autumn leaves in
November. Put your faith, your trust, your heart in the
very Christ of your Being, the One God, and there you
can feel peace, joy, harmony, perfection, even when the
outer picture on the material scene seems to be upsetting,

cruel, unjust. Hand in hand, let us walk. From The Christ Source, let us talk, feeling joyous, whole and free. Dwell forever One with Me.

Love, blessings, Amen.

#37 - Saturday

Dear Wonderful Reality; My God, My I AM Christ:

It is so great when I remember to follow the Principle; to relax on the Everlasting Arms; on the flow of divine life. Having seen through the illusion of humanhood, letting the presence, power and wisdom carry me on. I must not allow earthly imperfections to mesmerize me into believing in their reality. I give thanks for being admitted into the Kingdom of God.

I love Your Reality forever.

Dear Child:

As I speak to you and you write down, you are open and receptive and I feel that all is well with your so-called physical body; your activities and plans. Remember to relax; to let go of all concerns in the outer and to float along on the divine current leaving all up to God, His angelic Host, your Father. Have patience and forgiveness in your heart. Just grow with the inner realization that God is your life. God's life is so infinite, so beautiful, unchanging and eternal. Be at peace and rejoice, and be exceedingly glad.

Amen.

#38 - Tuesday

Dearest Indwelling Christ, My Reality:

There has been so much activity in the outer... cooking, entertaining, traveling, house chores, that my last couple of days have seemed too crowded to have our daily communication. Although in a motel, away from home, I AM alone with You. In quiet and in peace I listen to Your voice and teachings. My desire and prayer is perfect rapport with You so You can manifest through me and shine through me. I need You every hour.

While traveling in the car, while eating, while studying maps, I tried to tune in to You, but I miss our daily communion; alone with You, on my knees, my Dearly Beloved Counterpart. I love You and am so grateful for Your ever abiding presence.

Dearly Beloved Child:

You are guaranteed of My ever abiding presence. I will never leave you or forsake you, but what a loss to your spiritual progress if you do not find time to feel My presence, My love, My joy, My wisdom. So often man rushes about tither and yon... wearing himself out and needlessly feeling confused and frustrated when his life could be so orderly, perfect, successful, joyous.

For all he really needs to guide, to show the way, to reveal the rightful plan, is to get quiet, alone with Me, and all the joys of the Kingdom will rush forth to fill the vacuum induced by humanity.

Dear child, your life is enriched and glorious when you let Me live through you. Clear the way by putting Me first and all the other activities second.

#39 - Wednesday

Dearest Divine Partner:

The motel room is my sanctuary today and I kneel in the quiet and peace of my aloneness for our wonderful communication. Although the outer scene changes, I know that underneath all appearances is The Abiding Reality. Yesterday the pool was the scene of much exuberance, splashing, joyful and excited voices (even my husband and I were figures in such delightful activity later in the day). But today, because of rain and cloudy weather, the scene around the pool shifts to one of desertion and emptiness. How transient and changing are outer appearances, I give thanks to You that You are ever the same, always lovely, exciting, peaceful, joyful, true.

Dearly Beloved Co-Partner:

What a giant step is taken when one fully com-prehends the underlying Reality of God's unchanging presence, His light, love, are ever abiding and perfect. It is then that one knows that in Truth, his Christ Self , his Reality, is One with God's pervading Allness. The scenes played on this divine essence are the temporal, ever changing aspects. Although, in humanhood one seems to be part of this scene that changes from joy to dullness, from light and sunshine to gloom. In wisdom he should look through these appearances as Jesus recommended and behold the One Reality thus eliminating confusion, frustration, sorrow, defeat; no longer to be tossed back and forth like a ball from the seeming good to the seeming not so good, from happiness and joy to gloom and despair. Follow in your heart the Principle of

abiding **Truth which is constant, dependable, sure, perfect, loving.**

My grace, Amen.

#40 - Thursday

Dearest Divine Partner:
    How glorious to be back in the quiet of my home to
commune with You and learn of Your wonderful Truth. My
heart always overflows with gratitude for Your loving
presence and guidance wherever schedules and activities
may take me. My desire is to always keep in rapport with
You so the channel is open for Your life, light, wisdom to
come through to me.
    There are so many goings and comings in the outer;
which, if not understood, seem to deter me from continuing
on the narrow Christ Path. And so the announcement of the
arrival of another grandchild gives desire for Your interpre-
tation of meaning and significance. Your light is so illuminating. Shine through my consciousness and reveal the
Truth about life, birth, maturity, death.

My love and thanksgiving.

Dearly Beloved Co-Partner:
    **All is so simple when one comprehends the Truth
of Being. There is but One life... the life that is God life.
The life that knows no beginning, has no end or periods
of fluctuation and growth. This life is constant, unchanging, perfect, wise, beautiful. Although it is invisible to the
human eye, It permeates everywhere. It is instantly**

available, the very essence of All in the invisible. This One Allness, although invisible, expresses in a multitude of ways. It is like an infinite number of "Architects" with divine ideas from the One and same Source, producing multitudinous buildings.

Each Architect is an individual, an undivided entity, One with the All, yet producing its own structure. And so the Architect of this new life with its finished product in six or seven months, is working under divine Principle, and under wonderful wisdom and guidance. The product (baby) therefore, has a beginning, and what has a beginning must also have an ending.

The Architect releases into visibility, a manifestation of its great inner intelligence which has produced and shown forth Its mighty intelligence. The Architect is eternal (the Soul, the Overself, The Christ) and is the Reality of this manifestation of the baby and will continue to be the ever present sustenance and Reality of this manifestation as long as the rapport is maintained.

The individual Architect has produced perhaps infinite numbers of such products, visible on the human plane like an infinite series of beads on a string. But if a manifestation, like a bead, disappears from the human picture and is no more, the divine Architect, back of It, ever remains perfect, secure, immutable, because of Its being One with the Allness of God.

You have a divine Architect back of you. Each one has a divine Architect back of him, which is his true Reality. It is this Reality of you which you have been addressing and which is expressing through you, giving the Truth, revealing divine Principles. This was the Source which Jesus demonstrated. Isn't it gloriously wonderful to have what seemed to be an intricate puzzle solved and see how perfect, easy, beautiful It is!

Unless you ask, you do not receive. Unless you knock, the door will not be opened. Unless the student is ready, the Teacher will not be recognized.

My love, blessings, Amen.

#41 - Saturday

Dearest Divine Jesus Christ:

Everything seems so perfect and glorious today. The weather is sunshiny, yet cool, and I feel exuberant with joy and well being. Although I have much to accomplish, there is peace and happiness pervading my Being. It is one of those days when all is well and I give thanks to You for Your beauty, perfection and abiding presence.

Dearly Beloved Child:

It is a wonderfully glorious, beautiful day like this when you must be on guard and not go overboard on outer beauties and wonders. To be sure, you feel ecstasy in your heart because you know that the Source of this ecstatic joy is the abiding and ever permanent Kingdom of God. The pendulum of your feeling world will swing from great joy to utter despair because of dependence on the outer, transient, changing world. Do not allow conditions, circumstances, associations in the outer picture to move you from your Christ Center of poise, peace, harmony, which is constant, sure and dependable.

I know you have experienced this, because at times, when to outer appearances, there was cause for great distress and disturbance, you felt the peace that passeth all understanding and was moved and even filled with joy... joy of the eternal Spirit within. It takes constant disciplining to keep centered in your Christ Self, where peaceful joy, and ecstatic harmony, happy wholeness and divine perfection are always in balance and available.

The Father's Kingdom is yours. Already you are One with It. Enjoy the fruits of the Kingdom in calm acceptance and peaceful wisdom, knowing that the fruits, like the fruit of the apple tree are first the blossom, beautiful to see and sweet to smell, then the apples appearing to the eye and satisfying to the taste, then the tree undresses, its foliage falls, and stands bare to the shivering winds and wintry snows.

You can see the outer appearances change, but the Principle behind all this swinging of Its pendulum, is unchanging and dependable. Enjoy the fruits, giving thanks and praise to the Source and keeping your Divine Equilibrium, knowing the immutable Truth and wondrous Reality.

Abide in Me. Exult in My enduring presence. Live from the center out and your life will be poised, peaceful, righteous, filled with understanding, wisdom and peace that knows no end nor limitation. Isn't all this comforting to your soul and a delight to accept?!

Jesus always said, "Look through appearances." This Principle is to be applied whether what you are seeing through seems to be beautiful or ugly, good or bad, just or unjust. Thus you become a see-er, a seer in the true sense of the word and transcend Reality.

#42 - Tuesday

Dearly Beloved Jesus Christ:
    I give thanks and my love for seeing me through our time in St. Augustine. Why do I now experience such a let down? I realize the tremendous blessings when divine Principles and Truth are incorporated into my Being. This helps me to realize the depths of darkness so many go through, because, like me, perhaps they lost their hold on the link with God. May there be more compassion with them. Dear God, my prayer is to once again be so firmly allied with You that no segment of the physical shall have power over me.

My love and gratitude.

Dear Child:
    You do not stay in the valley, but only pass through it. I AM with you to lift you out of the depths of materiality and undergird you with love, strength, divine vision, so that once again you accept your spiritual Self and let God live for you. Surrender your hold on the lies of the physical world and emerge even more triumphantly than ever before. You are blessed and redeemed.

You are loved.

#43 - Wednesday

Dearly Beloved Reality, My Divine Angel:
    How wonderful to feel Your abiding presence and to know that we are One. There is no separation nor apartness

55

when I AM tuned in to You and see as God sees. In this realization of pure vision, I commune with You and await Your wondrous words.

With praise, love and gratitude.

Dearly Beloved One in My Oneness, My Allness:

It is only in false belief, not knowing nor understanding true Principles, that one can feel separated, apart, lonely, frustrated, unhappy. My Kingdom has come. Already, It is here and now, and the Real of you is Its eternal and glorious inhabitant. Now it is up to each one to see with spiritual vision this eternal Truth. Certainly mortal eyes cannot behold this Holy of Holies where All is whole, complete, pure, unchanging. Man's breath is in his nostrils and believes that only that which is revealed by his five senses is real. But this is not true.

Substance, divine essence, is the Reality back of all that appears and is the substance of the appearances. But do not judge by appearances. With greater illumination and Oneness with Me, the Truth is felt, perceived, accepted.

Unfolding spirituality, from sense to soul, is a mystical experience. This Principle can be seen in nature. For example, the birdling breaks through the bondage of its shell that has nourished it for a while and was a necessary step in its growth. But at the right time, it broke through its confines (although arduous this may have been, leaving it forlorn and weak for a while), it transcended this prison-like shell and found it had emerged into a wonderful new dimension of light and beauty, and it could fly. It was free, unlimited, and in song, could express this joy.

Truths can best be told in stories, parables , or relating to nature's programming. If the hidden, concealed Principle is grasped and felt, one will transcend his present dimension and arise from glory to glory.

Isn't it wonderful? Isn't it simple? Isn't it glorious? No one can know and feel the Reality and ecstasy of the Spirit until he follows the teachings of Jesus; the lessons of the Masters; the urging from the inner Self, and transcends into the ever present Realm of Reality. You, My disciple, are ready for these divine teachings. Keep them in your heart and let them expand into expression, knowing always that It is God... living you.

Love, blessings, Amen.

#44 - Sunday

Dearest Christ of Me, My Angel:
While away, I have missed this sacred time of communion. Likewise, have I missed the perfect realization of our divine Oneness. No longer am I satisfied to experience less than Your wholeness, peace, joy, harmony. Forgive me for these omissions and give me Your complete Self as I forfeit the lies and disagreements and in-harmonies of the mortal self. Through Your grace may I transcend the seeming shadows and dwell in Your illumination. Amen.

Dearly Beloved Child:
The doors are always open to My infinite and eternal heart, and as you enter, you will be assured that

not only has a place been prepared for you, but that already your Christ Self is dwelling therein, One with Me in perfection and harmony. This is to be recognized, identified with, felt, rejoiced in.

Amen.

The doors are always open to My Infinite and Eternal Heart.

#45 - Monday

Dearest Christ Self, ever awaiting my recognition:
I love You. You are my All and yet how often I let things of the world come between us. You are ever faithful and unchanging and it is this little personal self who fails to identify with You, that suffers and feels forlorn, separated, alone! Oh, how unhappy when I do not feel our Oneness. Only in perfect Oneness can You communicate with me. Teach me, guide me, illumine me.

My gratitude and love.

Dearly Beloved Child:
Already you are, now and always, One with Me. Know this Truth. Keep this alive in your heart. Already you are All that I AM, and in Truth, nothing else. Let down the so-called barriers of too much outer activity, tension, hurry, clutter! Keep simple, humble, relaxed. In Reality, there is no separation between us; you and I are One. But how unlikely and untrue this seems to be to man confined in and imprisoned by mortality. Break these chains, and Be! See the light, wherein there is no darkness. Let Me express through you. Hear My divine words, that all is well, here and now.

Love, blessings, Amen!

#46 - Tuesday

Dearly Beloved Angel of My Awareness:
When I went to bed last night I was both tired (from

baby sitting) and mentally upset by a long distance phone call. My sleep was not peaceful and I awakened with a sore throat. Dear Father, I know effect follows cause. I know this is the price to be paid for not forfeiting control, and not letting You, The Christ, rule. My prayer is to be back in harmony with You again, and to feel our perfect and divine Oneness.

My love and gratitude.

Dearly Beloved Child:
Troubles, anxieties, sleeplessness, weariness, are the results of falling asleep to one's true Reality and identity. You did not awaken to your true Self, The Christ, otherwise there would be no lack of harmony, wholeness, perfection, joy. Your thoughts keep reverting to your difficulty, the sore throat, but you should recognize the Truth that there is but One true throat, which is an integral part of the One complete idea in God's consciousness of the human body. The idea is the Real, eternal, unchanging, immutable, perfect. The outer picture is the One God, the only substance, this Truth of being is so easy to accept, and simple on the spiritual plane, but an enigma on the human level. Have faith in the teachings of Jesus, the Masters, the Prophets, the Seers, who know! Be One with them.
Jesus taught, "resist not." When something is presented to you on the material, the human plane, and you are not in accord with it, do not fight it. It is this which causes disturbance and can throw one off balance. Often when one takes the attitude "What is that to you, follow you Me," the pictures in the outer straighten out.

**It is like loosing one's grip, so there is freedom for things
to fall in place perfectly.**

**It requires mastership to resist not. It is so much
easier, and the human way, to try to fight and force one's
own mortal views and opinions. Just letting go demands
surrender of the temporal, and identifying with one's
own Reality. Only in this way can one keep in tune, to
continue to feel and express wholeness, harmony, peace,
and the feeling that All is well. Resisting is bondage.
Surrendering and being One with The Christ Self is
freedom. When you need Me, I AM there.**

Love, blessings, Amen.

#47 - Thursday

Dear Precious Jesus Christ:

I talk to You, the One and only Reality, as I would
talk to a friend, and I try to listen to Your words and advice.
This morning there has been a feeling of weariness, unrest,
upset. I didn't sleep well, as usual, and somehow I failed to
practice the Principle You so lovingly gave to me. I allowed
duties, engagements, plans to creep in and rob me of my
peace. It is important that I remain relaxed; that I allow
nothing in the outer to rob me of holding fast to the
Principle. I will pick myself up and start anew so joy and
fulfillment will take over. Help me in my endeavors.

My love and gratitude.

Dear Child:
The help you need must come from within you.

61

Discipline your thinking; feel relaxed floating on the divine current for underneath you are Everlasting Arms. Keep your thoughts in line with the Truth, always. Rejoice and be exceedingly glad that you have found the true Principle wherein you can breathe deeply and feel the glow and the inflow of God's presence.

#48 - Friday

Dearest Christ, My Very Own Redeemer and Helper:
I come to You primarily to feel our Oneness, that communication is open. I am receptive, to express my deep love and gratitude for You and to seek clarity, balance, peace! Give me illumination and guide me how to feel and react when unfoldments, conditions, decisions in the outer, that seem to be family, do not coincide with mine. I desire peace of mind, to relax, feeling that underneath are the Everlasting Arms. I know You are always with me, closer than words can convey, to align little me with The Christ Self . I listen, I write, I give thanks.

Dearly Beloved Child:
In the outer picture there are continued goings and comings. Change is inevitable. But just to see through all this passing show and beholding the One glorious Reality, is to find the peace, the stability, the joy, the wisdom of God Life. It is your, little personal mind that is judging the unfolding events and conditions in the outer and giving you feelings that are not in accord with God's immutable and eternal Self . Again, do not judge by appearances! What you see as possible trouble, disaster, defeat, could be the very avenue that

leads to the Kingdom of Heaven. **Learn to resist not. Let go. Do not hold onto the chains that bind. Your very resistance could hold back your loved ones' spiritual progress and rebirth. See all this as good. Feel in your heart that it is good, and a wonderful feeling of release and freedom will permeate your Being. Keep centered in The Christ; keep rapport with Me, your own divine angel and make a victory of what the senses label as possible defeat. God means this for good. Perhaps valuable lessons will be learned. Banish negation and live joyously, confidently, freely.**

Amen.

#49 - Saturday

Dearly Beloved Christ, The Angel of My Awareness:

As another day starts, I commune with You. Oh how wonderfully the day unfolds, how serene and peaceful the night's rest when I keep in tune with You. Truly, You live through me and express harmony, peace, wholeness. It seems the more clearly and constantly I feel Your presence, the more I crave of You.

Things in the outer are now assuming their proper perspective in the world of relativity. And so, although at this moment there appears to be a storm brewing, perhaps a tornado, I feel no evil for You are with me. What peace! What joy! What illumination... in the outer darkness of a morning's threatening storm! I have no need but You. I AM complete in our Oneness.

My thanks and love without end.

Dearly Beloved Child:

Keep open, relaxed, and receptive to My Reality, the only Reality there is. You are allowing the clutter of debris to fall away. What need is there in ashes, dust? Looking through to Reality is playing the game of life wisely, simply. You are learning the rules, and applying them. What joys unspeakable in knowing how to play the game successfully and being a winner. You know where the pitfalls lie and you transcend them. And so the seeming threat of a tornado brings no more alarm and fear to your consciousness than a calm sea on a moonlight night. Underneath, the essence is always the One, always the infinite, eternal, unchanging! Cling to this Truth and never be disturbed by lies and falsities.

Jesus calmed the storm by seeing through to this very Reality behind the appearance. Jesus healed the sick by the same method... One Principle for All... and for All times. Jesus knew the rules of the game of life, followed them closely, and endeavored to teach others. But these rules seemed not only so simple and childlike to others, but also so ridiculous, foolish, wrong, untrue to them. But I am teaching these rules, these divine Principles to you, and you are applying them, and when this is done consciously and constantly, you are having fun. It all seems so easy and perfect.

Do not be defeated; do not be a loser because of ignorance or because of unwillingness to play the game rightly. Also, you are not responsible for others who do not choose to play the game as Jesus taught. You and I are partners in this game and it becomes ever more exciting, thrilling and joyous. By my grace. I love you.

#50- Tuesday

Dearly Beloved Reality of Me, My I AM Christ:
        Togetherness again! A melting into divine Oneness!
I have pondered in my heart the teachings You gave
yesterday and had an opportunity to apply this lesson and
behold, it worked so wonderfully! My husband called late in
the afternoon. A business man from out of town was in his
office, and since I had dinner on its way, I invited this man
for dinner. Although the interval before their arrival home
was short, everything fell into place easily and almost
effortlessly. My attention was centered on the "now" activity. All was right at that moment. And the feeling of joy and
peace permeated by being and overflowed to our guest. How
grateful I am to my Christ, whom I love and adore.

Dearly Beloved Child:
        **Lessons are given to be used, applied, and how
much spiritual unfoldment is gained in this way! Living
in the now time and following through with step two and
three as given yesterday, is a wonderful formula! Banish
all doubts that perhaps by this method, there is not given
the right amount of planning for the future. Quite the
contrary! By applying the three point Principle there is a
screening out of all unnecessary thoughts, eliminating all
the clutter of muddled thinking. Only the necessary, the
vital, the helpful come through. Keep Your eye (I)
single... only... I AM... NOW! All is well!**

Love, Amen.

65

#51 - Wednesday

My Dear Precious Jesus:

So much is up to me to keep my thinking disciplined and in rhythm with the divine Truth. I always have something to do. I know the Principle works because things fall into place so easily, perfectly. I feel joyous yet so much is accomplished. I breathe deeply, automatically when this discipline is practiced. I am thankful for It.

I supremely love The Christ, God.

My Dear Child:

You are truly mine and One with my flock when you surrender the outer world of materiality in order to allow the God presence to flow into your consciousness. Then we are truly One and I can live through you as you. Life unfolds joyfully, easily, perfect when you abide in the secret of opening your consciousness so we are One. The Heavenly Host rejoices with you for having found the way; the Truth; the light. It is accepting the light wherein there is no darkness.

#52 - Thursday

Dearest Divine Self, The Christ of Me:

What joy in our coming together! What peace and understanding! You are the Truth, the salvation, the glory, the redeemer! When my heart stays unified with You, there are no problems, frustrations, worries! All is well! But too often during the day I allow things in the outer to take over my consciousness and rob me, seemingly, of this peace and tranquility. May I be so strengthened and firm in my convictions of Your indwelling presence and guidance that I will never more wander away in thoughts and become entangled in the web of third dimension confusion and shadows.

My deep love and gratitude to You.

Dearly Beloved Child:
Often when one awakens from a deep sleep, or dreaming, he finds himself in a state of partial wakefulness and partial sleep. There are lapses between being fully awake and half asleep. And so it is often with you and others in their journey from sense to soul, from unreality to Reality, from slumbering to being wide awake. When you become emotionally involved and over concerned with things, conditions, people, events, etc., in the outer, you are thrown off base from being centered in your complete and perfect Christ Self. You have allowed yourself to become partially hypnotized by the pictures on the TV or movie screen of humanhood, and so have wandered in consciousness, like the prodigal, to riotous living.

Things, events become out of proportion, out of focus; the now-time-living is projected into the future or falls back into the past. The secret as I have told you is to abide in the now-time, One with your Christ Reality. How else can communication take place unless we are in harmony, in rhythm, in Oneness! Life is to be lived beautifully, easily, fully, and this can only be realized by following the teachings of Jesus as I have been reiterating in these lessons. One with Me is the glorious answer.

If in consciousness you have strayed from the fold, awaken fully, and you will realize that already you are in the Kingdom of Heaven and that all is well. There are no problems that this Principle cannot solve; there are no untruths, that the Truth cannot annihilate; there are no shadows that the light of your own indwelling Christ cannot dissipate!

Love, blessings, Amen.

#53 - Friday

Dearest Divine Presence:

I come to You this morning with no requests, but just to feel Your wonderful Self so close to me, that my breath is Your breath, and Your love is the glorious joy that dwells in my heart. I come to thank You, for You have never failed me when I tuned in to You so perfectly that our channel of communication was not clogged by worries, frustrations and doubts or distorted by the clamors of the little self, the ego. With such freedom from all the synthetic opposites of You, our union is instantaneous and fulfilling. All the victories, the joys, the wholeness, the beauties, the harmonies and love that I have experienced in this life, I owe to You, for it has been Your Self living me, when I have invited and entertained You.

My love for You is surpassed only by Your love for me.

Dearly Beloved Divine Component, My Child:
It is wonderful when you have so disciplined and controlled the little self or ego, that it is not only willing,

but also delights in acquiescing to The Christ Self . Then there is no opposition. All works in harmony for the glory of God. When the little self surrenders, bows out, so to speak, the biggest obstacle to experiencing the Kingdom of God right here on earth, here and now, where you are, has been overcome. Jesus said, "I have overcome the world." He showed us The Way, but few are willing to follow in His footsteps. When the little self ceases to master, nor even has a desire to rule, The Christ Self is enthroned in the heart, and Christ Mastership is won. The ego then obeys joyously; equilibrium is gained; all unfolds in the Master Plan. Then your yoke is easy and your joys immeasurable. Truth reigneth; love rules, and life is without end.

My love and blessings, Amen.

#54 - Saturday

Dearest Father-Mother God, Divine Reality of Me:
        So very much do I welcome Your holy and loving presence this morning. You are a haven in a storm, an oasis in a parched desert. You are the fountain that refreshes and the peace that restores equilibrium and balance. Once again I reach out for You and find You are "closer than breathing and nearer than my hands and feet," for You are the true substance, the essence, of my Being. I feel merged, united, One with You. How then could I account for any other awareness than Your wholeness, joy and wisdom? You are truly All. Then all else that seems unlike You is no part of You and therefore temporal and fleeting. My consciousness is Your consciousness, and my life is Your life, pure and

unadulterated. Now I am seeing the Truth clearly and not through a dark glass. The mist is disappearing and I behold only You.

My love and gratitude.

Dearly Beloved Child:

When you tune in clearly to Me, the haze of clutter and confusion, doubts and discomforts, are gone. You see clearly and with understanding. I was with you last evening as you called forth special prayers to behold the living Christ in the little four-month-old child who has been labeled, since birth, with a mental shortcoming. You beheld the true Reality in this little one and saw so much beauty, sweetness, peace, shining forth through her. That little soul is calling forth infinite love and patience in her parents. Don't you see that she may be the very instrument to awaken them to a new world of abounding grace and divine love, lifting them to an awareness of a higher dimension in life which perhaps could not have been attained in any other way?

When this mission has been sufficiently fulfilled, normalcy will be evident in this little one and all will have profited. "God works in mysterious ways, His wonders to perform." Do not question; do not resist. Accept the beauty and love of this episode as an outshining of the inner Christ. I know you felt a Oneness with the life and Reality of this little girl. Spirit greeted Spirit, and neither one of you may know the raising of consciousness that resulted.

Look for Me in all the scenes of life and you will always find Me as a background, as a vital essence, with

**love to share, wisdom to teach, even through smallest
details, the light to illumine where there seems to be
darkness. Never forget my infinite love and blessings.**

Amen.

#55 - Sunday

Dearest Divine Partner, My very own Christ:
　　This is our time of communion; I push aside all else,
even though clamoring for attention. What could be more
important than keeping our rendezvous, where there is a
perfect blending, in Oneness. The sermon subject in church
this morning was Jesus' turning the water into wine at the
wedding feast. Unfold the meaning of this in my consciousness. Illumine me in Your divine Truths. I, Your servant,
take heed and listen!

My love for you is boundless.

Dearly Beloved Child:
　　**Jesus' consciousness was so beautifully One with
God, with Reality. His soul was so wedded with the Holy
Spirit, that this was the wedding, the union that he spoke
about in parable. When this nuptial feast is experienced
in the consciousness of God's children, something miraculous takes place. There is a transcending from the
water experience, to the wine experience; from third
dimension living to fourth... from the earthly realm
where the senses rule and command, to the Kingdom of
Heaven, where joy, harmony, beauty, peace, perfection,
reign in All God's glory. After going steady with The**

71

Ye are One with God.

Christ, after getting to know this loving presence, after being engaged in listening to His precepts, the holy marriage takes place, and there is the promise to live happily ever after in this divine Oneness.

Amen.

#56 - Monday

Dearest Lord of My Being, My Christ:

I greet You this warm and beautiful morning. Not only is sunshine "out there," but in my heart. This daily spiritual practicing, Your presence and communing with You has become the happiest and most joyfully anticipated time of my day. Practice makes perfect, whether it is learning to play the piano or violin or perfecting the play of golf, tennis, baseball, etc. And so this practice with You has made it so easy to feel Your presence anytime throughout the day or night.

I am learning to keep a more constant contact and awareness with You and it is so soul satisfying and glorious. It is like finding a tremendous fortune right at hand that has been there all the time, but could not be seen or touched because of a film over my eyes that concealed its presence. Through Your guidance, help, illumination, teachings, these so-called barriers, dams, films, separations, are being re- moved and I have found the treasure above all treasures, because You, Oh Lord, are the everlasting and infinite treasure, perfect, blameless, thrilling, yet soothing, com- plete... All!

I love You dearly.

Dearly Beloved Child:

You can remember how happy you are when your gift to someone has been accepted joyously, graciously, gratefully. The Christ is My gift to each and every child. It is so tender and precious, beyond price, because It is a part of Me, I have given of Myself, All I have, All I AM is the priceless gift to each and all. But too often this gift has not been recognized. Its presence has been obscured by the choice man has made to dwell in the world of things, of appearances... temporal, fleeting, changing. But when this no longer satisfies, as you have experienced, and the desire is so intense and sincere to look beyond the screen, the mist, the shadow of appearances, and find Me, the only Reality, behold the realization dawns that we are One and have always been undivided. This is the Truth. This is The Christmas message... to accept this glorious gift of The Christ, already abiding closer than breathing.

Through these meditations and communion times, you have been loving and nurturing this Christ Child and He has been growing into fullness of stature. The awareness of divine consciousness has been expanding until more and more of infinity is being your dwelling place. I AM always with you, and the Heavenly Host rejoices that you have accepted this gift of gifts and sing praises of thanksgiving to the One God. Your little ego has willingly humbled itself, and has become pure and in harmony with the scheme of God's wonderful plan for each of His children.

Unto each one, this child is ready to be born. Often, mankind has felt the pains that precede childbirth, but too often these birth pangs are misinterpreted, and thought and attention are focused on the world of things, rather than the awareness of the angels' message that a child, The Christ Child, is about to be born and His name is Wonderful Counselor.

My love and blessings, Amen.

#57 - Tuesday

Dearly Beloved Guardian Angel:
'Tis so sweet and quiet and calm for our communion time together. Would that this perfect peace pervade the day, which is scheduled to be so busy. At the start of this day, give me Your divine message. I await eagerly, prayerfully, joyfully, gratefully.

Dearly Beloved Child of My Perpetual Awareness:
How happy I am when I get through to you, which also results in your happiness, peace, fulfillment and wholeness, which you so much desire.
Even a toaster will not toast bread if not connected to the supply of electricity. So it is quite evident and simple that your life would be like distasteful bread if you do not continue to contact Me. There is ecstasy in Oneness. This is the true Intercourse, the results of which are always good, uplifting, joyous. You are My great concern. Your achievement of the divine Principles and holding onto them vitally, prove that My teachings are getting through and taking root. Be wise in these simple Truths! Nothing else is really important.
Isn't it wonderful to know that infinite wisdom, life, Truth, joy, is at your disposal to accept or in

ignorance, to reject? **But, be wise. And although even a trickle is better than nothing, let it flow freely, easily, abundantly so your cup runneth over and over floweth unto all you encounter. Keep up this Holy Communion. There is ever so much more to pour forth.**

Infinite love and blessings, Amen.

#58 - Monday

Dearly Beloved Reality, God:
    It has been a couple of months since writing in my Diary of Answered Prayers. But during that time I have lived successfully by following the Principle that all surroundings are unreal as a mirage; or pictures on a bubble that bursts and leaves only God Reality. This Reality immediately begins to function for me, even in the smallest detail. I just step aside and listen. I pray to continue in the illumination.

I give God my thanks and love.

Dear Child:
    Stay with the divine light. There is nothing, "no thing" to deter you since things have no power of themselves. How wise to place your love and attention where Truth and Reality are.

#59 - Thursday

Dearest Divine Presence of My Self:
    Would that I could feel close communication with You constantly and consciously throughout the day and

night as I experience during our daily communion time. I
know this lack is mine, not Yours, for You are constant,
unchanging, perpetual, never wavering an iota. Each morning at this time I remain still, my mind uncluttered and free,
so as to be an open channel to receive from Your abundant
and infinite good. Your blessings pour forth so richly and
abundantly that often I feel ashamed that I come to You to
receive but a thimble full, when in Truth, all of infinity is the
unbelievable receptacle. As I listen and write down, I know
not what is to be unfolded from Your immeasurable storehouse of All Good. I humbly listen and jot down, later to
study these gems of wisdom. I am so very grateful that the
"wires" of communication are intact. And may I ever
increase my ability to receive more. This is an opportunity
for me to discipline my little self; let it decrease so that the
Real Self of me can increase.

Silence, peace, gratitude, love.

Dearly Beloved, Sincere Seeker:
    **Truly I AM your ever helper, teacher, guardian,
healer and lover. Our Oneness is a precious Reality. I
want you to receive My perfect gifts... certainly not
material ones... but gifts of the Kingdom of Heaven;
poise, peace, wholeness, joy, wisdom, perfection!
Awaken completely from your mortal drowsiness. It is
only in carnal dreaming that there seems to be hurts of
the little self; indifference, lack of love, belittling, subtle
accusations, anxieties, frustrations. The little personal
self, the persona, wears these illusive garments to conceal, delude, hide, sidetrack your Reality.
    These negative feelings are signals, danger signs,**

77

that you must be on your alert to claim only your true, perfect Self , and to be very firm and adamant in letting go these false robes... "get You hence!" Go! Depart! Allow no adulteration of such ego centered feelings to separate you from the joys of the Holy of Holies, the Kingdom of Heaven. These negative tempters can be very subtle: Self righteousness, self pity, self glorification. It raises its nasty head so to speak, to try to get attention to divert your attention from the One. Thus you are immersed in duality. "Get you behind me"... this must be your creed in the face of these so-called devilish tempters. Keep centered in your Christ Self . This is your life saver. Do not let the little self cause you to drown in the sea of lies, half-Truths, self-pity, ignorance, etc.

Be Master! Be on guard! Grow! Be a light! It is in darkness where lurk the mirages, the ghosts that frighten, alarm, and tear you apart. This is My lesson for today! Apply it! Believe It! Treasure It! Keep It!

Love and blessings, Amen.

#60 - Friday

Dearest Guardian Angel, My very own Christ:
Such a late start this morning, (having gone to the garage, grocery, etc.) but it is not by omitting our precious communion time that I catch up with time and duties. Quite the contrary... I especially need this time of peace and quiet and communion with You to help untangle all the seeming snarls of activities and obligations. So I await Your wondrous help and wisdom.

Dearly Beloved Child:
Who seems to be so busy with worldly things and yet has the wisdom to get away, to feel the need to come apart, to pray, to commune, to get refilled with life's spiritual sustenance and to accept the help that is ever nigh.

I feel your gratitude for the perfect unfoldment and happiness of last evening's activities. 'Tis glorious when you listen and carry through. Then all falls in place so easily, perfectly and so joy-filled. Believe... there is never more to do than you have capacity to accomplish. If you feel weighted down it is because you are identifying with the little, mortal self which is pulled down with the gravity of mortal acceptance. But you can choose to be your true Christ Self... light, unweighted, free from the self-imposed shackles of living in the world of matter... filled with shadows, lies, discords.

Lift up your countenance unto Me and let Me provide the energy for each task, to decide your day's unfolding, to fill your Being with perfection, balance, wholeness, joy. Never be too busy to identify with your own Christ. Choose to serve Reality. Choose to live One with Me. Just relax, knowing that I AM! The Christ is your activity and joy.

Blessings, love, Amen.

#61 - Saturday

Dearest Angel of My Presence:
Happy communion time again! I invite! Come through, speak, guide, lighten my way! I know You are here,

I feel Your glorious Self and give thanks for Your wonderful guidance!

Dearly Beloved Child:
When as one becomes as a little child, one will become humble, receptive, expecting, innocent... in knowing the opposites of My whole and holy Kingdom. You are slowly becoming unselfed, loving simplicity, the joy from little, unexpected things. You are letting your intuitive, Real Self (I AM) supplant the mental self, using the intellect as a channel, rather than an end in itself. Do not be moved by what others think of you. Making this transition from self to soul is not easy and sometimes there is confusion and things are said either unnecessarily or without good judgment. Do try to improve, but do not let these remarks upset you. Remember, you are forfeiting the crumbs for the whole loaf of bread, so to speak.

Lessons must be learned along the way but I AM here to assist if you but seek and accept My guidance and help. My voice is low and tender, I will not intrude, nor force. So, often during the day, silence the clamor of the world and listen earnestly to Me. It is my delight to be accepted into the very depths of your Being.

My love is yours!

#62 - Sunday

How I love to commune with my I AM, God Reality:
...who understands me and my problems. It is good to relax with You, dear God, and confess my mistakes.

Yesterday, much time was spent reading books and articles. When already, I know the Truth that God is the One and only Reality; All love, peace, joy, wisdom, beauty, strength and that all else is fictitious, comes and goes, passing; therefore, unreal or illusions. This Truth is at the core of my Being. Why then should I search to get It from other sources? My attunement with my Christ Self, my spiritual reality was muddled last night. Therefore, my eternal Christ Self was not my functioning self, and so, with a feeling of being lost, and not being my Christ Self , the enjoyment of the evening was low. My prayer is to always be One with You, dear God and let go all else; then feelings of wholeness, health, joy, strength, peace, joy will prevail.

My love and thanks.

Dearest Child:
Upon arriving at a destination, it is not wise nor necessary to seek maps or directions to get there. And so, once having arrived, and loving the destination (a spiritual Being abiding in the Realm of Reality, spirituality with the Allness of God) all that is necessary is to give thanks for the guidance, the illumination in finding the Supreme God. Beyond which there is no other! Abide in this peaceful, beauty, resting haven, Heaven, and enjoy the friends of the Spirit. Blend with the All. Shine and be exceedingly glad.

Amen.

#63 - Monday

Dearest Divine Presence;

Togetherness time; holy communion, when the whole of me melts into the Allness of You. How wonderful to know and to feel that there is no separation between us, just Oneness, to let Your wonders circulate fully, joyously, perfectly throughout everywhere, including where my Being is. I thank You for this realization which only makes me ready and desirous for even a greater comprehension of Your spiritual Reality which includes me.

My love, my thanks.

Dearly Beloved Co-Partner:

Yes we are One. How could it be otherwise when My Oneness is the Allness! This is so simple, and yet so fundamental for happiness, wholeness, strength, order, peace. Dwell on this realization as often as possible. Cultivate a continual acceptance of this Truth, for in My Allness you are One with It. How could there be anything opposite to experience? My Kingdom, the perfect, everlasting spiritual Kingdom, is here and now and is the only Reality. Awaken and stay awake. This Truth is irrevocable, unchangeable, infinite and should be irresistible to you.

Jesus, The Christ, who taught this Truth and who lived It and exemplified It in every situation, is your Reality too. The Christ, this One Christ, is ever at your command to give of this Kingdom in accordance with your ability, desire, willingness to accept. "Ask and ye shall receive." Imagine, the entire Kingdom of Reality is

yours for the asking, and for the accepting. But the ruler
must always be The Christ. Otherwise, the Kingdom will
seem to disappear from your vision and experience. Let
The Christ take over. Know that of your little self
nothing can be accomplished. It is like a branch cut off
from the tree; it withers and is without sustenance. Live,
abide in this Real, wonderful Realm with Me and do not
wander away and sleepwalk; avoid unnecessary pitfalls.

Blessings always, Amen.

#64 - Tuesday

Dearest Father-Mother-God, My Divine Angel, Christ:
Communion time, away from my usual spot, but
down on my knees in this Kentucky motel as I seek Your
guidance and help.
The world seems to be in confusion and upset with
the President's announcement last night to put mines in the
harbors of North Vietnam to try to put an end to this war.
Dear God, enlighten me as to the meaning of all this. How
can I keep spiritually in tune with You constantly and
consciously? I await Your wisdom.

Dearly Beloved Child:
**Conflicts are a part of the mortal scene. All is like
a nightmare because of being immersed in materiality
which is like a curtain closing off the Real. It isn't easy
to be in the world but not of it. But it is important to keep
constant vigilance where you regard Reality to be All
and to choose to serve the Real.**

If you were watching a battle on the movie screen, how foolish it would be for you to be terrorized, emotionally disturbed and sick because of viewing the play of light and shadows on the screen. When you realize that all this is taking place on the screen you can remain peaceful and calm and composed.

And so when you perceive My unchanging Kingdom, the only Reality, where all is perfection, harmony, peace, you, in your wisdom, will not allow appearances to disturb you. Keep anchored in the Truth of Reality which never passes away, in contrast with the mortal scene which is ever changing and passing. You have nothing to fear with Me at the helm. Do not be disturbed for you are a spiritual Being in Truth, upheld, supported, by My spiritual Principles. Choose to serve Me constantly, unfalteringly, wholly and joyously.

Amen.

#65 - Wednesday

Dearest Guardian of My Self, My Very Christ Self:
Alone with You, but away from my usual sanctuary. Communicate Your wisdom to me. Teach me again and again that which is necessary for my good, my wholeness, my happiness. It is my desire to always live close to You, to partake of Your spiritual feast. No more do I want the crumbs of half Truths that only delude and dissatisfy. Come forth, speak. I love You as the infinite Reality and yet my individual guide.

My Greatest love to You.

Dearly Beloved Seeker of even more Truth:

I hear your plea and am more willing to satisfy your hunger than you could possible imagine. Most important is the Truth that you know, accept, have faith in and trust that I AM. How pitiful and what pitfalls, unnecessary of course, when My children do not even recognize My presence... that I AM Real, in fact the only Reality.

You have accomplished step one. I know you feel My abiding presence, have faith and trust in Me. Also, you can ask whatever you will to receive of My Kingdom and you will receive abundantly. But, remember, I can only give true gifts... of spiritual Reality. Ask Me for wholeness, for peace, for harmony, for love, for life, for wisdom, for joy, and you have already made a channel, so to speak, for these blessings to pour forth. If, however, you ask for things that are of the world, as a good and trusting Father, I could not give you shadows, phantoms, make-believe mirages. Trust Me, request wisely, being not concerned nor deluded by the passing things, and your satisfaction will be full. You will enjoy the ephemeral things, knowing their true illusive nature, but you will not be unhappy if you do not have them.

My Kingdom is the Everlasting Kingdom and is yours for the asking and receiving. Do not be dissuaded by those in darkness who are ignorant of these steps. But be a light unto them, which will help their shadows to be thrown behind them... (to Satan... get you behind).

This is a big lesson to master, and to receive your Mastership you must discipline self and pass the test. You are doing well as evidenced by your feeling of peace, well being, joy. The Christ of you is as a mother loving her child. I want you to experience Heaven on earth.

You are loved.

#66 - Thursday

Dear Divine Christ Angel:
    Communion time today is as the day closes, not as it begins. However, I felt Your precious presence ever with me as this busy day progressed. All went well and I thank You for going ahead to prepare parking spaces, select my purchases, etc. How could I ever feel alone with You by my side!

Dearly Beloved Child:
    The world is good, the people so good, cooperative and helpful, as you have found today. Through your mouth, appreciative and admiring words were spoken to your waitress this noon, which helped give her what her soul needed. Remember her remark, "You have made my day." It is I, The Christ, who makes each day beautiful, glorious, harmonious, loving, an adventure in finding Reality, which is always within one's consciousness.
    Remember, even if a day seems filled with activities, always there is room to recognize My presence. As springtime bursts forth there are so many wonders that suggest, hint of My Being as the cause of their being. All is One. Delight in this Truth. Feel light and buoyant. Feel the glory of good and God.

My Love and blessings, Amen.

You have made My day.

#67 - Sunday

Dearest Christ Reality, Me:

Today is Mother's Day and I have invited my mother, dad, Dot, plus other family folk. I do not know at this time if they will come because of how they feel, rainy weather, etc. But You know what is best for today's unfoldment and I want Your will to be mine. Clear for me what my attitude should be towards family. Enlighten me in the Truth about relationships here on earth. I am so grateful for Your guidance.

With deepest love.

Dearly Beloved Child:

Yes, I have been addressing you as my child. Doesn't that prove then, that I AM your Mother and Father? I address the Real of you, and certainly The Christ of you is My eternal and perfect offspring... My son, My daughter, My child. And so this is like unto Me and as your parent, you inherit All that I AM. The whole Kingdom is yours... but only as long as you believe you are the child of God and live and act and abide in this realization.

It has been said, "Call no man on earth your father or mother." And how true to Principle, for you have an eternal Father and Mother whose love for you never changes or dies. It is the Real of You, your eternal Christ Self , One with God, that produced the temporal you, which, as you know, is only a shadow of the Real. Mortal man, the carnal earthly mother and father can do nothing of themselves. How could they produce an eye, an ear, even one hair? How could they set up a mechanism, even a temporal one, that breathes, has life, energy, etc.?

The answer is simple... they could not. Once again, these material manifestations (mortal bodies, flowers, trees, mountains, oceans, stars, etc.) are but symbols that God has extended into visibility, to give a nudge to the wise and to the alert, to look behind this outer scene to the inner cause, to the One God. All this gives a hint, a clue to the wise to uncover, to unveil the outer appearances and behold what is behind: the Real God, the Real you, The Christ. Perhaps hidden from the ignorant, but there in All Its perfection and Oneness for ever and ever. Isn't it wonderfully glorious when you see the whole Truth?!

As for your mortal parents, they deserve the love, the recognition, the appreciation for the part they have played in your behalf on this mortal scene. They have cared for and provided for you as best they knew how. But they should not be worshiped as creators, or regarded as idols, just as it would be wrong for your children to look upon you thusly, for this would be sinning against the One God and breaking a commandment. For in Truth, God is All. I AM the One. Do not let your feelings be diverted into byways. Keep your vision single and do not get sidetracked because of mortal holidays or celebrations.

Be free from half-Truths and falsehoods. Keep life simple, easy and joyous. Every day will be Mother's Day and Father's Day when you commune with the One Real Father-Mother-God daily and let this eternal, infinite I AM be at the center, the hub and the circumference of your life. This is the only true relationship that you should accept. If you allow yourself to get entangled in any other, you will miss the mark (sin) and the price to be paid is too high (gloom, unhappiness, disharmony, unwholeness). Live One with Principle. Let go all other enticing attitudes. My love is a true mother's love for you!

#68 - Tuesday

Dearest Angel of My Being, My Christ:

Beloved, how wonderful and comforting it is to come to You for holy communing each day, to get my spiritual food to sustain me and give me strength, comfort and courage. Certainly, little on this material plane is joy fulfilling. I must transcend its pictures of dualism for there seems to be lack of harmony, lack of patience and coopera- tion, lack of love and compassion, not only on the personal level, but also on the national scene (shooting of Governor Wallace) and on the world arena... wars, conflict. How futile and grievous the expression of life would be, if in my ignorance, I would accept the mortal scenes as true, Real, as I know Reality. The Truth is immutable, unchanging, perfect Principle.

Dearly beloved sustaining presence, I need to abide in You, to rise above third dimension existing and to live at right angles to it, in the Kingdom of Heaven, which is here and now. Oh that I would always keep my mind and heart open to this Truth, and not allow my senses to lull me into a coma of unreality. I must keep awake to the Truth by living as One with You.

Oh great Master, teacher, and guide, I love You and am grateful to You for keeping me in balance in order to let the rest of the world go dizzily on its frantic course if it chooses not to put You first, now and always. You are my inheritance, my life insurance, my love, my All.

Dearly Beloved Disciple:

I feel your earnest desire to abide in the Realm of Truth with Me. I can see how you are disciplining Self

not to accept the ephemeral, though tempting, as the lasting, final Reality. I AM with You to give You assurance, strength, light, love, peace, and a happiness that transcends human understanding right in the midst of human frailties, perplexities, confusion. You must see through this fog of mortal drama and delusion in order to remain fully awake to where your true place is in the Kingdom of Heaven, here and now.

Do not give outer tragedies, disappointments, lacks, the power to change your emotions from those like unto Me, to feelings that are unlike Me. Principle never changes. Do not swing between Principle and untruths and be as a house divided. And as has been said, you cannot mix oil and water. Life is simple, beautiful, holy and glorious only in proportions as you abide with Me. To all else say, "What is that to me? I am determined to follow The Christ." Let the rest of the world go by; let the lies be crossed out and crucified; let the ego be destroyed all over the world; let the mortal pictures fade out, and then a "New World" that has always been and always will be, come forth, be seen, be recognized. Let go and let me, The Christ of you, shine in all Its glory and righteousness. Be adamant, be sincere, be pure in heart, be victorious, be The Christ of your Being. All the angelic Hosts are at your hand. Alleluia!

Amen!

#69 - Thursday

Dearest Angel, aware of My Self, My Christ Self:
Happy communion again (here in a trailer). But

wherever I AM, You are! I am sure that there is a ratio between my keeping in contact with You, and with my harmonious unfolding. Would that this communion could be more constant and conscious!

Just one week from today is a big challenge (Argus), but I know that You prepare the way and take care of all the big and little details. I thank You for being my guide, teacher, helper, wholeness.

Thank You, Heavenly Father.

Dearly Beloved Child:
Since you are an essential and integral part of Me, how could we ever be separated in time and space? All of My wisdom, energy, is available for you if you but accept and believe.

To be sure, you seem to have little discouragements in your personal activities, but as long as you know, believe these are but shadows seen on the eternal screen (for the eternal screen is the essence, the light, without which these shadows could not be), you will not be touched or moved!

Never feel neglected. Never indulge in self-pity, for I am flooding you with love, so what else matters? Keep centered, keep poised, keep calm, keep happy. Know in your heart that "All is well" for God is All. All else is a seeming, a passing show. My love for you is infinite and eternal.

Amen.

#70 - Friday

Dearest Christ, My Redeemer:

And today I really need redeeming, for I have allowed persons and circumstances in the outer to throw me off base. I have been like the prodigal and in spite of all my intentions and desires, I have wandered from my Christ Center and the result has been lack of joy, lack of perfect well-being, lack of poise and relaxation. Forgive me, God, I have been tempted by the devil of carnality and have succumbed. Pull me out of these doldrums immediately. I surrender my All to You for You should be my only concern, interest, and abiding place. Illuminate me so that all darkness is dissipated.

I love You above all else!

Dearly Beloved Wanderer:

Not truly lost, but temporarily you have lost track of Me, The Christ. There could be no misgivings, no worries, no upsets, no disharmonies, no real displeasures when you are awake and aware of Me, The Christ! I have been pulling, like a magnet, to retrieve you from the pitfalls, to prevent your falling into the abyss of negativity.

Sometimes mortals get a strange kind of satisfaction, a false pleasure, from immersing themselves into self-pity, self-glorification, self-righteousness. But remember, whenever the little self, the little ego, is in the driver's seat, you are heading straight for destruction, unhappiness, hurts, frustrations, perplexities, problems! No problem can be rightly solved when this ego is using

its little, temporal mind of the illusive senses! Always this leads to something other than 2 x 2 = 4.

Of course, you are forgiven the moment you surrender this false self with all its subtle maneuverings, plots, schemes. I am waiting to welcome you, to receive you to the Kingdom of Heaven, from which you really have not left but except in your imaginings. Shed this illusive veil. Be free from all involvements with the devil. No longer be tempted. Keep centered in Me and be willing to accept results, which, to be sure, must always be like unto Me.

With love that never ceases, Amen.

#71 - Saturday

Dear Divine Eternal Presence and Power:
Had a very busy morning yesterday. But sitting outside this afternoon, I could feel Your wonderful, loving presence, such peace and relaxation! But this morning, my husband awoke greatly disturbed and angry with the pump. So there is need for feeling a renewal of Your presence and power and love. Guide me! Illumine me! Help me to be guided through moving plans. I thank You and love You supremely.

Dear Child:
The outer is opposite to God, since it is passing, ephemeral, unreal. If you fall in conscious, this three dimensional Satan, or devil, can seem to test you. So do not fall prey and be its victim. Keep One with Reality and you can even say "to hell" with all opposites. Let go

as if you were touching a burning something. Do not get
burned by the devil which is all illusion, anyway. Keep
on the straight and narrow Christ Way of Reality. Do
not give in to opposites, lies, etc. I AM with you always to
sustain, soothe, lead, guide and to love you (do not expect
love from the outer).

Amen.

#72 - Sunday

Dearest Reality of My Being, My Christ:
      Speak dearly beloved, Your servant listens. It is time
again for our spiritual communication and a seeking for an
answer. The big news of great concern and anxiety is the
destruction and flooding caused by hurricane Agnes. Thousands of people are homeless and damage is enormous. I
know You are perfection and peace and harmony and beauty.
How can all this destruction and calamity be explained?

      My love and gratitude to You are infinite.

Dearly Beloved Child:
      **The Father's Kingdom of Reality, which is here
and now, and everywhere, is perfect, harmonious, beautiful, and is immutable, indestructible, eternal, infinite.
It transcends the seeming picture of humanhood which
is ever in a state of flux. Changing in its duality from
what seems to be good to what seems to be bad, from so-
called beauty to ugliness. This transient seeming is like
the pictures on a TV or movie screen where only lights
and shadows, passing scenes and pictures can cause one**

to laugh, to cry, to be anxious and concerned.

But all these pictures are playing on the screen, which in itself, is changeless. The spiritual Truths must be perceived spiritually. Metaphors, parables and the like are sometimes helpful when translated into their hidden meanings and Truths. Jesus taught to see through appearances, and behold Reality; not to let one's gaze stop with the human picture. As for man whose breath is in his nostrils (the pictures on the TV screen)... why be mindful of him who is like the chaff which the wind blows away?

Jesus presented one illustration, one parable after another to illustrate this Reality. When humankind plants seeds of humanhood, the harvest is that of humanity. Principle never deviates. When man's chief concerns in life relate to that of mortal man (what he should eat, what he should drink, wherewithal should he be clothed), he is allowing himself to be closed off from the Kingdom of Heaven, even though the Kingdom is nearer than breathing, and closer than hands and feet. When one blocks himself from the breathing of air, he strangles himself, suffocates, perishes, even though air is everywhere.

Man needs to be awakened from falsehood! In his ignorance he has planted seeds that produce storms, troubles, anxieties. And yet these catastrophes, if looked upon positively, can awaken him from his mortal existence. A good shaking will arouse man from his deepest sleep. If man would be wise, he would know to put his trust, his faith, his love, his attention on that which is Real, abiding, beautiful. If all man would so live, the Kingdom of Heaven would be experienced right here on

earth... "on earth as it is in Heaven." When one is wide
awake, he need not be awakened. It is that simple. Glory
in this eternal Truth, dear child. It is so wonderful and
Real!

#73 - Monday

Dearest Christ Presence, My Own True Reality:
    Anchored to You, I feel no evil... I am safe, secure,
loved, watched over, yet free to be, and to express You
wholly, joyfully, radiantly.
    I come to You with this so-called problem, just to
release it, and to hand it over to You to handle. It is but three
days before Argus Club picnic here and this morning the
pump refuses to flush the three toilets. I know that in Truth,
all is well as it will be on Thursday. I do not shut off Your
divine ideas and help by panicking, feeling upset or concerned. And so it is. But my thanks and love for You is
infinite and I AM abiding under Your wing, under Your
tender care.

Dearly Beloved Child:
    **If you were to see an enactment of this so-called
crisis on television you would not be one bit touched or
concerned... (you couldn't care less). Even looking back
on your own life, these critical situations even seem
laughable and so very unimportant. Assume this attitude now and do not forfeit your divine Mastery to
unnecessary and ridiculous slavery. So what? All that
should concern you is to keep the Principles I have
taught you, alive and uppermost in your consciousness.
    Do not let caustic remarks of others even make a**

dent on your consciousness. **Forgive, forget, and see through this outer scene of make believe. I AM at the root, The Source, the essence of All. Call on Me as you have this morning. Surrender your problems and concerns; do not keep them to yourself where they seem to multiply under Your heated attention and concern. Let go. Have fun. Rejoice! Make each moment special by seeing My presence and My activity. Only good is My promise to you. Accept.**

Love divine and blessings, Amen.

#74 - Tuesday

Dearly Beloved Christ, My Own Angel:

I come to You later in the day, weary from much toil (getting ready for Argus Club -Thursday) and tied up with material things (cleaning, preparing salad, etc.). And so I need Your tranquil Spirit to comfort and soothe me and put me back into balance, when as Your child and heir, I AM already. How quickly we can allow things of the world to push in and cloud our vision. I thank You for Your constancy and ever abiding love and help.

Dearly Beloved Child:

You are not too tired to hear Me and jot down as I speak. In the twinkling of an eye you can feel rejuvenated, rested, renewed when you return to Me in consciousness. How can My love, strength, joy flow through you when you have built a separation block of materiality? To be sure I AM everywhere equally present, but when you fall asleep, lulled by mortal nightmares, it

98

seems that My presence is divided. Relax and let go all concern in the outer. Have faith that I am taking over for you. I AM to be the hostess Thursday and by your willing surrender you are allowing your guests to feel My presence, My love, My harmony, My beauty. Isn't this a glorious gift? Just accept and be free from all concern and anxiety. I love to live through you.

By grace and love, Amen.

#75 - Wednesday

Dearest Divine Angel of My Awareness:
       How wonderful to know and feel that You are ever awaiting my turning to You in quiet communion. Always You are with me as soon as I fulfill my part to tune in. You are more wonderful by far than anything mortal eye can see, or carnal mind can comprehend. And this wonder of wonders; that You never stray, diminish, nor forget me, but are constant, sure, dependable, infinite and eternal. What a marvelous heritage of goodness! And I am so very grateful to be Your child and to have this relationship and rapport.

My love! My thanks!

Dearly Beloved Divine Counterpart:
       For that is what you are in Truth and in Reality. We operate as One and always this operating is becoming more smooth, harmonious, effective and glorious. Oh how joyous I am to not only give you the Kingdom, but also to reign and rule for you.
       You have no worries nor concerns about tomor-

row. Whether you have ten or twenty five guests, all will unfold smoothly, joyously and perfectly. Each one, if receptive, will receive a special blessing, for the vibrations in your home are very high. These guests will feel My presence, light and love, and if they seem to need a healing, suddenly they will feel whole. If they seem to have problems, the solution will be right there. If they have allowed the perplexities and shadows of materiality to darken their horizons, suddenly a new light will shine from within their very own souls and dissipate the gloom and shadows. What a shrine of healing, renewing, regenerating you have called forth in your surroundings by allowing Me to be Your "Chief Occupant and Householder." I am rejoicing in tomorrow's opportunities for the spreading of the spiritual Kingdom.

Love, blessings, Amen.

#76 - Thursday

Dearest Father-Mother-Christ of Me:

This is the day I have worked toward for almost a year. At first I held this with anxious anticipation, some worry and doubt (of which I regret now). This has been like climbing a mountain and now reaching the summit. We are blessed with a most beautiful day and all seems to be unfolding well. But I want so much to feel Your wondrous presence right here with me every moment of this day, and always, to be sure. May I keep calm, poised, efficient, joyous, radiant with Your love. Please be my very Special Guest and may each guest receive Your special blessings! I am so grateful for all Your help, inspiration, guidance.

Dearly Beloved Child:
I have already accepted your invitation. In fact I AM always present whether you know it or not, whether you have invited Me or not. But the Heavenly Host rejoices at your recognition and gratitude. I AM your constant help and servant to do as you desire as long as it is in tune with Me. This can be one of the best days of your life. Just let it be and rejoice! I AM with you. Relax as you go along and receive My ideas.

Love and blessings, Amen.

#77 -Friday

Dearly Beloved Co-Partner, My Angel Christ:
This is the day after and thanks be to You, all went smoothly and well yesterday. The number was much fewer than I had expected but perhaps that was Your way of facilitating and easing the activities of the day. And even when it was time to retire at night, I did not feel the least bit weary or fatigued. In fact, to the contrary; I felt exhilarated, rejoiceful and relaxed. I know it was Your strength that flowed so easily and abundantly through me and performed all the tasks. Also I feel that Your loving Spirit permeated everywhere, and the group felt renewed, happy and sure that it was worthwhile making the trip out here even if some did get lost on the way. My love for You is infinite.

Love and gratitude.

Dearly Beloved Partner:
I love you and it is My joy to help you constantly.

101

You may never know the good that some of your guests felt penetrating throughout their Being yesterday. I was happy to be in your midst, as I will be Sunday, for your next hurdle. Remember, I AM always present. Wherever you are, I AM. But on those special occasions you open your consciousness even wider, and think of Me more sincerely and consciously so that even a greater flow bursts forth. You know if you go to the ocean with only a thimble to bring back water, that tiny amount is all you will be able to hold. And if you go with a gallon container, you can lay hold of many times more. And yet the waters in the ocean are immeasurable as is My love and blessings that I am so eager to pour out upon you.

The rapport, the relationship, the Oneness of us is becoming even more beautiful and Real. I can feel your sincerity and deep devotion to Me, the One Cause, the One Reality, and it is ever increasing while your hold on things of the earth is decreasing. This does not mean that these earthly things will be taken away or disappear, but when you graduate to this dimension where you know that things of the world are results, effects, coming and going, of transient nature, you can enjoy them in a more true way. And the vacuum that this produces makes room for even more blessings to rush into your experience. But always remember to keep in your heart the Reality and livingness of My Kingdom. Then all these things will be added at the proper time and in the right way. I love you as a disciple, even as Jesus Christ loved his apostles.

You are loved.

#78 - Saturday

Dearly Beloved Angel, My Reality:

My thanks to You could never be adequately expressed, and my love for You is infinite. May our rapport
never be severed (and if it is, my personal little self would be
the cause of the disconnecting). May our Oneness be ever
more greatly felt by me, and when I let You take over, what
wonderful healings come through. How or when, I do not
know and cannot explain. All I know is I have an awareness
of Your wonderful presence and I let this divine Reality take
over and live through me. I am so grateful, so filled with the
ecstasy of Your presence, My cup runneth over.

Dearly Beloved Offspring of My Love:

**Yes, you can have Heaven on earth when you
tune in to My presence and the Kingdom of Reality and
feel the Oneness, this is All there really is. Why get lost
and confused, bewildered, unhappy and weak by wandering away in consciousness to that which is not... to
that which is just a seeming, a semblance, the world of
appearances with all its lies and shadows? Be in the
world but stay wide awake, like knowing in a dream that
it is only a dream and that in Truth you are safe and
sound on your bed.**

**I would like to lead you to greater expressions but
you must first discount all doubts and lack of your
capabilities (which are really My talents, capabilities).
Listen attentively to My guidance and ideas which will
lead you on paths that I have already prepared for you.
After a banquet has been prepared you don't just sit and
look at it or say how beautiful it is. To have a complete**

realization of it, you must partake of its essence, take it away from its apartness on the banquet table, and let it be assimilated as a part of you, lost in your Oneness.

And so it is with these lessons I have so lovingly prepared for you which have been spread out on the banquet table of your consciousness. You have been assimilating them, but now they must be shared with all who are hungering for such delicious spiritual food. I know you do not know how this can be accomplished, but the answer is about to be given you, so be calm, poised, expectant, receptive and joyful. You are My tool, My channel, My vehicle through which I express. Such Wonders of Wonders are about to be born, craving for expression. Do not stifle and have a stillborn. I AM with you always. Keep ever aware.

Love and blessings, Amen.

#79 - Monday

Dearly Beloved Reality:

My great gratitude for the divine Principle. The thought came this morning to direct my breath to where it can do healing, make perfect... One with God. Following this Principle has brought restful nights sleep, a feeling of relaxation, joy, peace, almost exuberance. Oh dear God, my thanks, and help me to continue with this divine, healing, beautiful Principle.

Much gratitude.

My Dear Child:
When you seek and are receptive and thankful, God Reality pours into your Being via your breath. Deep breathing gets you in tune with God, with Reality, and you become One with the All, which is the purpose of your life's experience.

#80 - Tuesday

Dearest Angel of My Awareness, My Very Own Christ:
Now at the conclusion of a three-day holiday and two parties of our hosting, I feel back in the groove again. Just one more hurdle (Thursday's Symposium in Louisville). Today, after weeks of sunshine and fair weather, it is cloudy and rainy and it seems to be so relaxing and cozy. Great thanks need to be expressed to You for Your ever loving help and wisdom. I could feel Your presence and Your soothing guidance which serves to guarantee me continual help as long as I stay in harmony with You. Please teach me more; I yearn for greater illumination and more of Your love above everything else.

Gratitude plus.

Dearly Beloved Student, My Very Own Unfolding Self:
Yes, I have been aware of your requests and even before you asked, fulfillment was at hand. Most of the time you have accepted but there were times when you were blind to the banquet spread before you and cried for crumbs. Such is humanhood. But this false, erroneous state must be transcended. The little self must die so that you can be reborn into the Kingdom of Heaven as

soon as you awaken from mortal sleep. Dear child, do not slumber in ignorance and falsehood. Be One with My infinite, wholeness, joy, beauty, wisdom, harmony. All is yours for the acceptance but it is impossible to accept while your vision is darkened with the lies of mortal appearances which are as a screen hiding My wonderful Realm. Pierce this bubble of illusion and by My grace you will dwell as one of the angels. Your own angel is guiding you to live as One with God, although still expressing on earth. Let your light shine, your spiritual, true eternal light... certainly not your mortal false seeming. Claim your heritage. Be free from false-hoods, hurts, criticism, condemnation! As long as you are looking toward humanhood for your soul's satisfac-tion and happiness, you will be frustrated and miserable. You, in your humanhood, cannot satisfy others, nor even yourself. Graduate out of humanhood. Your diploma is at hand.

I need you, as you need Me, Spirit, to Spirit... to have wholeness and completeness. Divine love is so wonderful and fulfilling and there is no place where this is lacking. Do not be your own enemy that makes you a prisoner... when in Truth, you are free and One with All Reality. Believe this, beloved student, It is the Truth.

My infinite love and blessings, Amen.

#81 - Wednesday

Dearest Angel, My Very Own Christ:
This is our special communion time, this time in the Executive Inn, Louisville, Kentucky. All is very plush and

beautiful here (our first stay in such a glamorous motel). The third, big hurdle is to take place tomorrow when my husband, Dick, has his symposium. I am so grateful for all the harmonious unfolding and I know Your divine presence will be felt, as always.

My infinite thanks.

Dearly Beloved Child:
   Never allow material grandeur to be put on a pedestal. Remember: The things of beauty of today are but ashes tomorrow. But always look through the appearances, whether of elaborateness or simplicity, to the essence back of all. That is the unchanging Reality and the eternal essence, and when this is perceived in your heart, it should result in ecstatic emotions. The kindling of beauty is an inner realization and is not dependent on outer circumstances, conditions, or things. The One resides behind all appearances and this beauty never fades nor turns to ashes. Keep alert to the abiding Reality and do not allow even outward beauty and harmony to form a film over the true and Real.

My love and blessings, Amen.

#82 - Friday

Dearest Angel, My Very Own Christ:
   Yesterday was the third hurdle. The day was beautiful, the attendance at the symposium was quite good, and the sessions unfolded satisfactorily. For all this I give thanks... that it was under Your divine supervision. However, my day

was so busy that I hardly had a moment alone. Our communion time was practically nil. The day seemed cluttered with people, conversations, foods, etc., and perhaps cluttered with emotions involved with humanhood. I want so much to return to my wonderful rapport with You and to feel calm, peaceful, whole and joyful again.

Dearly Beloved Child:

All these outer activities in the world could be regarded as the uppermost of a mathematical fraction, varying, changing, etc., but always the common denominator should be the same... the One, infinite, unchanging Reality. Surface activities can proceed in this human scene, but always you should feel that beneath are the Everlasting Arms on which All outer scenes rest. Do not allow these two to get mixed up. Each has its place and should be regarded rightly.

The fact that you felt very weary and exhausted at the end of yesterday indicated an adulteration in your consciousness of the temporal and eternal, the illusive and the Real. Be your own master, or rather, let The Christ of you master each situation in which you find yourself. Then calmness, peace, joy will prevail. You are here to learn and it is a gradual, unfolding process to human consciousness. To the divine consciousness the fields are already white with harvest... all is perfection, harmony, bliss.

My love and blessings, Amen.

#83 - Saturday

Dearest Christ, My Co-Partner:

This is our special time together, when I completely let go all concerns about the outer and feel only Your presence. You are my only concern and joy right now; all else is released, vanquished, unimportant. My love for You is complete. You are my All.

The lesson I desire for You to reveal to me this morning is that of true wealth. On the Today Show there was conversation about protecting one's estate from probate so that more will be left for the inheritors. There was a talk about wills and what part the government plays in death taxes. Illumine me with Your true light. Set me straight. I listen now... only to You.

My love and thanks are infinite.

Dearly Beloved Child:

How often we have spoken of My Heavenly Kingdom as the only true Reality and that each one is heir to this Kingdom as my child here and now and always. Please believe... the only true wealth of any value is this Kingdom of Reality where God reigns. All else that seems to be wealth is only counterfeit, fictitious, an imitation.

One must take a step in a higher dimension, transcending what seems to be wealth on the earthly three dimension plane of the senses of man whose breath is in his nostrils. This mortal, personal man who has a birth date and a death date often foolishly seeks his riches on the earth plane. He tries to count his wealth in

his accumulation of bank accounts, stocks, bonds, lands, material possessions, and calls all this his. And yet at the time of his death all this material wealth is no more his and all must be forfeited, left behind. And yet, during his life span he had a choice to determine where true wealth lies. And certainly it should be clear to him that which is not eternal is only on the relative plane, that of the human or mortal. But what a glorious career it would be to be about His Father's Business where true riches abound, and are infinite and eternal.

While on earth, which is a training ground, one should engage in this wonderful business, have communion with the "Head of this Concern," the eternal God, and let Him run it for him. These riches, which are in divine consciousness, are unfolded ever more and more as one turns to Jesus Christ and claims wealth that is eternal. This is putting first things first. This is returning to the Source, the storehouse of eternal riches, which, when accepted, felt, can never be taken away, stolen, lost.

There is a Principle involved: when one thus lives according to the teachings of Jesus, The Christ. He feels his Oneness with The Eternal, and releases concern over the riches of this outer world. There is a flow of this three dimension wealth coming forth, which, to humanity, seems to be wealth. But never misidentify true wealth. Do not misinterpret. And when your first aim, objective, goal in life, is to awaken to, to enter into, the riches of your divine inheritance, and care little whether much or little is manifest in this world, you will never lack, never be in need. This Principle is simple, and It is simply wonderful, fulfilling, full of rich blessings.

#84 -Tuesday

Dearest Divine Angel, My Guardian Christ:
How grateful I am that You are ever present with me... nearer and dearer than any earthly kin could ever be. You are ever ready to fulfill my every need. In Truth, "already the fields are white with harvest." Already in Spirit and in Reality, fulfillment already Is. How wonderful to perceive that my true habitation is complete, beautiful, harmonious, peaceful, and already a place has been prepared for me.

It is my desire, that while still expressing on the earthly plane, to succeed in living One with cause, One with God, in the Kingdom of Reality. How easy then, to let the effects, the results, fall where they may, regarding them in their true light as transient, passing; although, at the same time, not disregarding, nor ignoring them. Thank you, my angel, teach me more.

Dearly Beloved Counterpart:
Such rejoicing in Heaven when even one soul sees the light and knows the Truth that eradicates ignorance, and feels the peace that passeth all understanding. What a beautiful relationship! We need each other and yet we are One.

With the eyes of Spirit you look through the veil of materialism and behold that which abides forever. With the consciousness of Spirit, you transcend third dimension limitations and live and love and breathe the very atmosphere of the divine. Your mind is thus trained to tune in on immortal ideas that seek your acceptance. Your whole being is aglow with the radiance of the

divine. All who come within your aura, if receptive, should feel this divine Reality, much like a flowering bush gives off perfume that fills the atmosphere. And this very fragrance could alert passers by to the very Source and cause of this outward display of beauty and fragrance.

Your Divine Self

Divine love is so wonderful and fulfilling,
and there is no place where this is lacking.

All this is so subtle and yet so very simple. Do not cloud the Real by any thoughts, feelings, attitudes unlike that of The Christ. Jesus was such a perfect example of living in tune with God, and how easily miracles were performed through Him. Get your attention off the fleeting, the changing, the temporals which are but symbols, suggesting, leading one to the true Realm of Reality. Master this Principle and you shall always be Master of your life.

Love divine and blessings, Amen.

#85 - Wednesday

Dearest Lord of My Being, Beloved One:

How greatly I anticipate this quiet communion time with You each morning. It seems that when I am down on my knees (and facing the East), our communion is more clear and I am more receptive. How grateful I am that this time of rapport in meditating and writing has been established as a daily adventure. So much good has flowed through; washing away all the old debris of self thoughts and feelings and opening up into an infinity of All perfection. May I grow and unfold ever more like unto You.

May guidance be given as to how to use these lessons that have come through so lovingly, easily and helpfully. Sometimes it seems selfish for me to keep these hidden and to myself, when perhaps others could profit by them... to help others lift the veils that conceal Your abiding presence and glory. If I am to share these Principles of Truths, these meditations, these questions and answers, please lead me to the way of outlet... I know not how. To be sure, there is no intent to glorify my little self because it was only through transcending this third dimension of materiality that Your teachings could come through. Perhaps anonymously would be the way to use these... with all praise, glory and thanksgiving being given to You.

Dearly Beloved Outlet of My Self:
     Nothing that is divine, nothing that is God-given, nothing that is perfect and true can be hidden forever. Ultimately it rises to the top, much as cream rises above the milk. These lessons are "tops" in the Absolute, the Ultimate, but would have no appeal, no understanding to many... those who have not been searching and thirsting for Truth as have you. However, for those who are ready and eager, there is a channel already open, to be used. Relax, have confidence that you are becoming aware of Its presence.
     This Truth is needed in the world. The time is about ripe. Do not fear that your personal self will erroneously be glamorized. If you had not already humbled yourself, had not already graduated to the higher dimension where our Oneness is felt, and our rapport is active, brilliant, vital, gloriously satisfying, these lessons would never have unfolded. The Christ is the Reality of your Being and is the author of all the good flowing in and through our Being. If you maintain this Truth in your heart, you need never be concerned that the little personal self will be erroneously glorified.
     I AM showing you the way. Be alert. Follow through. Every step, I AM with you to illumine the way so you need never stumble, nor fall. Blessings, by My love, and by My grace you are guided.

#86 - Thursday

Dearest Christ, Angel of My Being:
　　Together let us partake again of Your wonders, Your perfect Kingdom of Realities. I would be ever more like You. I invite You so fervently to live through me. I desire so greatly to have Your ideas flow through to my awareness.

　　　　　　　　Gratitude and love fill my whole being.

Dearly Beloved Child:
　　We are One! There is no separation in Truth. You are becoming a more open channel so that this Oneness can be realized. Constant disciplining is necessary until it becomes not only a habit, but also a very joy and delight of your livingness.
　　Wholeness, harmony, perfection, order, beauty... this is your heritage. I AM your real father, mother, guardian, teacher, companion, more Real than any in the so-called material realm. There is no limitation to the divine gifts for you as long as you remain receptive to receive, and aware of and open to My presence.
　　This is living gloriously, easily, joyously. My light is illuminating your way right now! My ideas are permeating your being right now! My perfection is All there is of you. Nothing else matters. How could a no-thing have power? Delight in the Law of the Lord. Sing of these joys in your heart always. Become less and less involved with appearances, humanhood, the passing show. The Truth is needed by all to bring Utopia (Kingdom of Heaven) here and now. I feel our rapport.

#87 - Saturday

Dearest Angel of My Awareness:

Greetings to my constant companion. This is the happiest time of day. What joy when You are speaking through me and directing my way. You help me transcend this little self and rise into the true Realm of Being, prepared for me from the beginning, my true dwelling place. Speak to me, give me more of Your wonders and glories for which I am so very grateful and filled with love for You.

Dearly Beloved Child:

If you were the only one in this entire Universe, you could not be given more awareness, more help, more love, more guidance than is being bestowed on you right now. And as this is divine Principle, it is certainly true of each and every one in this universe. How wise to be aware of this Truth and to open up to this Reality and to feel One with the All. You were meant to be an expression on this earthly sphere, of All that the Father Is. Let your light shine forth. Do not have feelings of inadequacy, that others are more gifted, talented, capable than you. How could that be when you know the Truth about yourself? Feel when you are expressing that it is not the little personal you, but your very Christ expressing and that the little you is but the channel or instrument necessary, of course, but not the end in itself, to be sure. Have confidence in this inner Christ Self , against which there is no opposition.

My love, blessings, and by My grace you have transcended into an awareness of your own Christ.

#88 - Sunday

Dearest Christ, My Redeemer:

Here I AM, in Your very presence. Such glorious communication, such beautiful partnership. Hold me like unto Yourself, fill my consciousness with Your divine ideas. Be a light unto my way. You are so very real, gentle, all loving, and wise. My gratitude is deep, my love is unspeakable.

Dearly Beloved Redeemed Child:
You have been reborn, no longer of the earth (earthly), although, at times you yearn for humanhood's expressions and even feel you are being neglected, forgotten! But when you have grown to adulthood, no longer do you need a pacifier or children's toys. You have outgrown the limitations of three dimensional materialism and are reborn, this time to your spiritual identity. This is where and how we communicate. On the human plane this is not possible.

But you are not to ignore humanhood any more than you should be asked to ignore television because this only portrays pictures, not the flesh and blood performers. Be its master and do not be mastered by it. The Christ is your King and Master, in Truth, and always with you to guide and help.

Live abundantly, freely, joyously! The glory of the Lord is your heritage. No good can ever be withheld. You have broken through the veils and we see each other face to face. This is real, true and wonderful. By My grace you have been redeemed.

117

#89 - Monday

Dearest Father-Mother, My Very Own Christ:
Company is coming in a couple of hours and there is still much to do, but how can I forget You when You are not only my Guest of Honor, but also the host (and hostess).
Somehow this morning when I started to make preparations I could feel Your presence of joy. I know that You are delighted to work through me to prepare and entertain for this luncheon. In being aware of Your loving help, I AM so completely unburdened, that I invite You to continue to take over and I will be Your assistant. How wonderful You are.

My deep gratitude.

Dearly Beloved Co-Hostess:
You are My extension, My Being. The All of Me is available to you. I do so rejoice in hostessing this party. Remember we are All One. Just as steam is the invisible state of water and ice the visible, although in essence the same, so in Truth we are One, but expressing in variation. Although unseen, I AM as Real as the seen, only much more infinite and so very eternal. I AM at your right hand, to serve. Thanks for allowing me to be your Guest of Honor. I love you and cherish this friendship.

#90 - Tuesday

Dearest Father-Mother, My Christ:
Keeping in tune with You, trying to be ever aware of Your abiding presence is the most wonderful and stabilizing

influence and privilege of my life. Yesterday You were my Host. You were right in our midst when I entertained. I wonder if Your joy was as full and complete, even when I wandered away in consciousness from You. My desire is to glorify You, certainly not to neglect or hurt.

Also, was I being disciplined? Did I have a lesson to learn... when one of my objectives in having a very neat house was to see that the toilet bowls were spic and span and then to have dirty well water that left a filthy deposit?

There are many questions unanswered. I need at times, a clearer focusing into Your wonderful Reality. But always I am so grateful and so filled with love for You.

My love and gratitude.

Dearly Beloved Child:

These experiences come into your life, not to chastise nor to punish you, but they are opportunities to gauge your spiritual growth and development. As has so often been said, it is not so much what happens to you in your daily life experiences that are important, but it is your reaction that is so very crucial. Your choice of reaction can either make you (help you to unfold even more gloriously in divine consciousness) or break you by taking the path of the prodigal and wandering away in consciousness from Principle and from the ever present glories of the Kingdom of God.

You said you hoped you passed this test yesterday and indeed you have. Your example may help your guests to apply similar reactions to things that seem to come to spoil and upset.

The sharp corners are being smoothed and

rounded. You are growing stronger spiritually and when you choose to follow the way Jesus taught, the entire Heavenly Host is at your command. We delight in your progress and unfoldment.

The dirty toilet waters were really pure cleansings and were meant for good, not evil. My student is trying and succeeding to pass into the next grade.

As to My joy and happiness, It is always complete and unchanging. How can the eternal waver, change, or be less than all good? But your human joy is in proportion to your awareness of divine joy or bliss. There is a transcending process in which you return to the Real Source and cause of All, God, which never fluctuates. Do not judge by effects, results in the outer world. Abide with Me as I AM forever abiding with you and experience love divine.

Blessings, Amen.

#91 - Wednesday

Dearest Divine Presence:

I greet You with all my heart. My love for You is beyond expression. Oh, how I am trying to keep consciously and constantly aware of Your Holy presence. And how utterly helpless, weak, annoyed, upset I seem to be when I allow a fear or anxiety to bombard my consciousness. And how, when I dwell on this disturbance, the ill feelings seem to multiply... all its aunts, uncles, cousins seem to rush in to have a picnic at my expense. And yet I know in Truth that all I need do is to turn to You, my divine presence, and this seeming host of enemies will flee away. They have not a leg to stand on, when Your light and Truth are recognized and I know that I AM One with You. Such has been my recent experience. Oh divine redeemer, how grateful I am to You!

Dearly Beloved "Redeemed:"

In Truth you are as whole, complete, perfect, harmonious as I AM, for we are One. But there seems to be a battle raging whenever this Principle is forgotten. Already you are redeemed forever and ever, but there is a seeming need for redeeming whenever one of my children forgets, or falls asleep in mortal dreaming. And the nightmares can seem to be so terrifying and ugly. See how important it is to stay awake to the Real and perfect? Always keep so alert that your foundation will be secure and you are well-grounded and strong against seeming storms and apparent disasters that would upset and throw you off balance.

In Truth there are not two powers... God and the devil (ego). There is only One Real power, activity, force, presence and each one of God's children is One with the Allness of that power and presence. Abiding in this consciousness, one is safe, secure, free, joyous. But to deviate from this Truth is to invite trouble which humanity calls the devil... Satan.

(2 X 2 = 4)... This is Principle, unchanging, Real, true, everlasting, no matter in what language it is written or by what tongue it is spoken. But 2 X 2 = 5, or 3, or anything other than 4, is a lie... Satan is a liar. The Bible teaches this. And what a host of troubles will picnic in this dilemma when one has made an incorrect equation. Do not blame the principle of mathematics, nor the multiplication table when you have used it wrongly, or

interpreted it erroneously. And never... in like token... can God be blamed when we disregard His Principle of Truth that I keep giving to you.

And so when you felt upset yesterday you can be sure you were wandering away in thought, feeling, consciousness, from the Truth of Being. But all you needed to do was to turn again to Me and with out-stretched arms, I take you to My bosom. And I am as patient with you as an earthly mother is when her little child falls while learning to walk, and caresses her hurts and bruises. I love You. That never changes. Always I AM right with you. And there you find peace, relaxation, fulfillment, wholeness, joy. The Father's Kingdom is pure delight, indescribable wonders and you are abiding in this glory of glories right now. Cease from wander-ings. Keep alert. This is simple, but demands constant vigilance.

Love divine, Amen.

#92 - Thursday

Dearest Angel of My Divine Awareness:

How wonderful to commune with You again in the silence and tranquility of my own room. Much activity has been enacted on the outer scene and I am grateful for harmonious unfolding. But with it all I have allowed myself to wander at times into the byways with the result that my attunement with You needs to be cleared and perfected. This is my prayer... may I receive Your whole Self , may I be receptive and feel our Oneness. I love You supremely.

Dearly Beloved Child:

How great shall be your reward when communion with Me shall not depend on place, environment, persons, circumstances, conditions. Always I AM with you, offering you All that I AM. But when you do not claim your divine heritage... the very Kingdom that surrounds you, and is the only Reality, you feel weakened, frustrated, lonely, apart.

As the current carries the leaf safely around the obstacle, so are you floating on a Divine Current that knows where it is going and how. It is supporting, as long as you relax and "let go."

But I AM the unchanging, always at your side and your command. It is up to you to keep this rapport, this Holy Communion, alive, uppermost, constantly and consciously. Keep your life simple and uncluttered. Nothing should be so important that this spiritual communion should be neglected and pushed into the background.

My light is always shining. My love is always active. My divine ideas are always flowing. My wholeness is always complete. And all of this is yours for the asking and claiming. Feel that there is no delineation nor boundaries between us, that All is Oneness. Relax from humanhood into the glory of My Everlasting Arms that uphold, sustain and soothe and carry you on victoriously and effortlessly into the right expressions and experiences at all times.

This is much like floating on a divine current that knows where It is going and how It is supporting, as long as you relax and let go. How else could you float? To sink would be the neglecting to see and to apply this divine Principle. Don't go down when you can stay on top. On top of all your seeming problems and perplexities. I shall make your burdens light and your day's unfolding happy, peaceful and fulfilling. I love this time of communion, I know I am getting through and I have faith in you as you have faith in Me.

Blessings, love, Amen.

#93 - Sunday

Dear One God, One Power, One Presence:
How grateful I am for all the blessings You have

bestowed upon me throughout my life. Today is my sister's birthday and I am so thankful for her and love her. Guide my step to do right by her. Your guidance, love, illumination is needed greatly by me, for my grace is very low... lost in a desert, a wilderness, the valley. My prayer is for help and healing, to overcome Dr. K's verdict, to overcome upset over a recent dress purchase. My prayer is to be lifted out of the wilderness, to be rescued from mortal webs, to once again, feel that I AM The Christ, One with Your eternal Allness and wisdom. Help me to emerge from this dark tunnel and once again to see Your light and feel Your presence. You have been my guide and savior in the past. Take my hand, my body, by mind, and melt all discordant conditions into Your beautiful and perfect Oneness.

My love always, and great gratitude.

Dear Child:
   You are not lost. Open your spiritual eyes and behold the One eternal Kingdom which is the All. Do not think that you are residing in another world, for this is the fictitious, shadowy world of unreality. I AM God, One with your I AM Christ, as with Jesus, The Christ, who overcame the world. Choose ye now the Realm of Reality. Shift from falsity into Reality. Know that the unchanging, eternal Kingdom of God is your habitation. Do not be deterred by human frailness. I AM with you always to be One with... Me... the One God, the only power.

You are loved.

#94 - Wednesday

Dearly Beloved Reality, My I AM. One with God:
    I start another notebook this morning and Dick and I
begin our second half century of married life. There is much
to do the next few days but my prayer is to be in perfect
alignment with God Reality and to be this eternal, spiritual
One... to feel peace, power, wisdom, light. I thank my dear
Real One. Be with me.

My love.

Dear Child:
    **All is unfolding according to God's perfect plan. I
see you as your perfect Christ Self. One with God's
Allness. Have no fear of anything in the physical world
(people, plans, your body). Relax on my Everlasting
Arms and be at peace. Know that you are loved.**

#95 - Saturday

Dear Wonderful, God Presence:
    My sustaining guiding reality, making all things
perfect. My love and thanks to You for the two wonderful
children you formed within me and for the five wonderful
grandchildren. Thank You for helping them along their
journey. You have given me divine Principles that have
renewed and nurtured me. Give me now, the One beyond all
others that I can always keep in my consciousness.

My great love and gratitude, always.

Dear Child:
My true disciple who has accepted My love, guidance and illumination. The unseen, the invisible, ever present God is the only Reality and you are made in His image and likeness. Therefore, the Real you is invisible and One with the Allness of God. The out working of the invisible God is seen on the earthly plane to be cherished and loved, but not as the Source. For the Source of God is unchanging, perfect beauty. Whereas His handiwork changes and passes away, and yet since God is One, the only presence and power is God. His essence is the Reality within all appearances and the substance of what appears. Rely on and be One with God only. Look through appearances and behold the One and identify with your true, eternal Self.

#96 - Wednesday

Dearly Beloved God:
My thanks to Jesus Christ... One with my eternal, spiritual, I AM. How wonderfully well You have prepared the way to guide me through the business of parties and guests. I am blessed with joy, strength and fulfillment of every kind. Lead me on to express adequate gratitude and to follow Your wonderful Principle. I thank You for peace, energy, wholeness, joy and all Your great gifts of children, grandchildren and most of all, my precious husband. Illumine me even more as I progress and try to follow in the footsteps of Jesus Christ.

My everlasting love and gratitude.

Dear Child:
  Your soul glows as one of the stars and is illuminating your pathway. You have endeavored to follow the precepts given to you and all is well as your life unfolds before you. You shine forever in joy, inspiration strength and peace. Keep aware of God's ever presence and take pleasure in His abundant gifts.

Amen.

#97 - Friday

Dearly Beloved Christ of Me:
  Once again I welcome my sacred and glorious rendezvous with You, the Reality of Me. May my theme this morning be divine ideas... to know their presence, to accept and to act on them. In the silence, once again, I await Your perfect illumination.

I am eternally grateful.

Dearly Beloved Child:
  There is no division between all true ideas. There is no separating them, no limiting. All are available to you. And as you meditate and ask confidently to receive the ideas most helpful to you and needed by you, they gravitate towards your awareness. All that I have is thine. I know your needs; what is best for you, before you even ask. I watch over you. I want you to receive your good. Yours as My heir through Jesus Christ who is your Reality.
  The best ideas are the most simple. When compli-

cations and frustrations seem to be, just let go everything and start anew with simple childlike trust and patient joyfulness, confident that your help is right where you are.

Divine ideas cannot be selfish. They must be for all times and all people. They are products of Principle. I will feed into your consciousness these ideas, one by one as you remain calm and peaceful. Expect, receive, act.

My love and blessing, Amen.

#98 - Monday

Dearly Beloved God Reality:

I know it takes daily practice and discipline to see through the mirage of earthly life and align with the One, all pervading Reality wherein is forever my I AM, my true Reality. And when I AM in the flow of Truth, all unfolds easily and well. It is very important that I abide in this Principle for there is much for me to do... especially in the next two weeks before we leave for two weeks in Canada. I must keep calm and relax on the flowing current and feel Your peace.

With great love and appreciation.

Dear Child:

Don't be too serious even if your tasks are many. Try to feel light, buoyant and joyous. All is well in the kingdom of God Reality. Do not judge the changing pictures that come and go. Know your center of Reality, your I AM, and abide One with It. What is all this

changing panorama to you after all? It's like a passing
dream. Awake and be The Christ now and always. If you
can see it, it's not forever.

#99 - Wednesday

Dearly Beloved, Eternal God. My I AM Christ:
I hold onto You and my Oneness with You as a
drowning man would hold onto his life preserver. You are
my sustainer, my guide, my strength and Truth. There has
been much activity in the outer, but I regard all life as a
passing show on which I can look. But I see its temporal,
passing, ephemeral illusion. I must not allow myself to get
caught up in the web of the temporal, the false. Guide me
through the week of baby sitting and to do all I can for my
sister before we leave for Canada. I thank You and love
You. My true Father-Mother God.

How I love and praise Your holy name.

Dear Child:
**You have found the eternal Truth and who you
really are. Never get side-tracked into the byways of
earthly reality which is an illusion. Keep aware of my
presence and love for you. I will never leave nor forsake
you. Keep relaxed and floating on the current of divine
love, allowing this Reality to live through you as you are
as perfect and whole as God. For you are Spirit, The
Christ Self . Know that you are loved.**

Amen.

#100 - Saturday

Dearly Beloved Reality. My Real Self... One With God:
    My prayer, my plea, my desire is to find again my
eternal, true spiritual entity. Somewhere I got lost and what
trials ensued (blood shot eye, rash on my nose, fatigue).
With all my heart, I seek the everlasting Real Kingdom and
my Real, eternal Self which has lived through me and for
me the past months. I yearn to be reinstated to full divine
activity, love, joy, peace and enthusiasm. Cleanse me from
all secret faults. I ask for forgiveness if there are things to be
forgiven. I open myself to You and praise Your glory and
Your holy name.

                                            I love You.

My Beloved Child:
    **You have hit bottom, perhaps, but only in belief.
Awaken from your mortal dreaming. All is well. Perfection reigns and God never changes nor does your Real,
eternal, spiritual entity. Be relaxed without mortal concerns and obligations, Let go of all earthly illusions and
mirages. Be light, love, beauty and peace.**

#101 - Sunday

Dearly Beloved Divine Presence:
    Come through to me. Teach me that which I should
know. May my consciousness ever unfold higher and higher
to receive Your Truths and abiding precepts. Perfection,
wholeness, happiness, a complete awareness of You. This is
my goal. I come to You uninhibited, eager, enthused and

awaiting Your discourse.

Thank you from the All of my Being.

Dearly Beloved Child:
You are ever admitting more light and this more easily and joyously. This requires a lifting of consciousness away from mortal falsehoods and your awareness. Peace reigneth. Realizations tumble into your awareness. Soon you will realize that you are One with perfection, for you will identify so completely with your true and perfect Reality that always was and ever will be. Even when things are easy, perfect and joyous, continue with Me and our divine rendezvous. There is always more light to brighten your way, and more to unfold. Whenever you need a new precept, there I AM to give It to you.

Keep relaxed and trouble free. Let nothing disturb you. Feel as calm as a mirrorlike lake, but with deep depths. Love everyone and everything. Pour forth this blessing on all; let it exude; let it escape like an uncorked perfume bottle.

Remember that all the good that is pouring forth into your acceptance and realization is for the purpose of bringing Heaven on earth right here and now. You are My channel. Never block it with any negative feeling. Our love for each other is mutual. Never forget me.

You have taken many difficult steps upward in search of Me and now you are ready to fulfill your desire for wholeness, joy, life, harmony, peace, glory. Truly, there is no turning back. What you have gained is forever.

I thank you for being My ready, willing and receptive pupil. We are One. I AM you and will always express if you come to Me and request It, humbly and sincerely as you are now.

My love and blessing, Amen.

#102 - Monday

Dear Jesus Christ, My I AM Reality:
I love you and thank you for taking over for me. My desire is to identify more completely with You and to really be my eternal, spiritual entity; One with You, here and now. Some of my mortal problems have come to pass. My eye is almost back to normal, but there is a breaking out on my nose. May these appear to disappear and already I thank You. The number of things to do after returning from the north is beginning to decrease. I thank You for being my true Self.

Love always.

Dear Child:
You must always go back to Principle. The One Truth as Jesus taught here on earth and what so few understood. But you must accept it completely and to the exclusion of all else. The underlying essence that cannot be seen or felt by humanity is everywhere equally present. Powerful even in the most distant of places and deepest depths it is constant, eternal, perfect. The Christ essence is the only Reality and your true Self is One with It. So, all else must be a seeming, an illusion. Appear-

ances, like shadows, can fool you to believe what is not true. So the imperfection on your nose, your eye, the body are to be regarded as nothing. But always be aware of who you are. You are a spiritual, perfect Self.

One with God.

#103 - Thursday

Dearest Helper, Guide, Instructor, My Christ:
Once again, communication! And how I need You to help me with my divine attunement. When I get off the track I yearn for divine adjustment. I desire to maintain the Single Eye, beholding and living the One Reality, always. Set me free from all that is not in divine order. It seems that I cry out so often to be shown the way. You are so patient with me. I need this contact with Reality. Illumine me! Instruct me in the thoughts, feelings and attitudes I should cultivate. I know You hear me, and now I listen to Your loving and redemptive guidance. I love You.

Dearly Beloved Child:
You are trying so hard; perhaps too hard. The Truth is already within you. God, the unchanging, the immutable, All love, All good, All wisdom, All harmony, All perfection, is All there is. All else is just a seeming. This Truth was instantly grasped by you many, many years ago which resulted in instant wholeness. This same Principle works now. Law is unchanging. Don't let appearances rule you, for you will certainly then get off track.
Appearances in the outer are like a mist that

hides the Real. You know that a mist is like a shadow, a cloud, a reflection on the water. Just a picture that appears to disappear. Place no power nor credence in this. As you go through your day, be in command. Ally yourself with the Truth, The Christ. See through the mist; through all the changing scenes and behold the One Reality; God, the I AM, your Christ. Hold your head high. You are above lies. The Truth has been given to you. You must believe! Be free, not a prisoner of false beliefs... the devil... the so-called opposites.

See yourself as the perfect creative idea in God's mind. Let go the pictures that deceive. Be firm. Be brave. Be illumined. I will, and can help you if you maintain this Principle. "Be Ye perfect, even as your Father which is in Heaven is perfect." (Matthew 5:48) So-called healing comes as a result of following this Principle. I want to help you as greatly as you need Me. Let there be a blending of Oneness. Already I can hear your soul joyfully crying out; "I thank You Oh God, Oh Christ within for delivering me from evil; for dissipating all darkness; for making clear the Truths, the Principles that work to bring great peace, joy and wholeness."

My love and blessings, Amen

#104 - Monday

Dearly Beloved Presence:
How grateful I am that I am aware of Your unfailing Beingness! How I want to open the channel between us even more, so that more of Your illumination, wisdom, guidance, can come through. Always, when my way seems darkest,

He Talks With Me

light breaks forth and dissipates the gloom and frustration.

Your three point "secret" came forth upon my awakening yesterday morning. There You were, so willing to help and solve life's mysteries. All the little segments of Truth fit together by Your wisdom and made the three-in-one... Trinity... the perfect, complete answer. I have practiced these separately... now I see each is a step and a vital part in spiritual realization:

(1) This (here and now circumstances) too, shall pass into memory, perhaps to be completely forgotten.

(2) I see through this dreamlike mirage surrounding the here and now, which later will be like last night's dream... just an appearance, a picture, like on a bubble about to break. By seeing through, I AM a seer.

(3) I see through this passing scene to the One and All Reality which I AM. I am synchronized with God.

All is in harmonious working together. The Father and I are One. This is the ultimate goal and the absolute Truth of Being.

Thank you, Father, for this revelation.

Dearly Beloved Disciple:
You are so teachable, so willing to learn and to apply what I have revealed. These three steps can, and should be, realized as one. In a twinkling of an eye, you can see through the passing picture before you and see into your true Self. The only Reality; so perfectly harmonized and beautiful; so peaceful, loving and good.

Of course, the first step is very important. It gets you off the ground so to speak. You realize the Truth about the appearances that you are presently facing.

136

This must be surrendered. Its transient, ephemeral shadow speaks of illusion. Once you get off the ground by being wise, a seer, you abide in consciousness where you truly are in the eternal, unchanging God, the Kingdom of Heaven.

You are united into Oneness where there is no beginning, no ending, no outline, no separation; just a perfect blending. Then your God Self takes over. It is speaking to you now from the Realm of Truth. All the saints (Jesus, Buddha, etc.) are blended into this presence and are with you now.

Keep centered in this Truth of Being and our help to you will be immeasurable, infinite, perfect, wise, loving, All Good. Through persistence and faith you have found the secret which, if applied, will always unlock the doors of the Kingdom.

You have nothing to fear when you abide in this secret place of the most high. Wholeness and perfection reign in the outer, passing scene (the mortal body, surroundings, etc.) as reflections, shadows to be sure, but symbols of the inner. Go in peace, dear one. Relax with gratitude in your heart with glory and light shining forth from your happy soul.

My love is yours, Amen.

#105 - Tuesday

Dear Wonderful Reality:

Yesterday, I affirmed The Principle that I learned so long ago. I learned that in order to behold the One God I must dematerialize all in the outer world. I must see through the mirage and illusions and be One with Reality. Somehow, this true Principle relaxed me so. My breathing is slower and calmer and I feel that I am on the right course... following in the footsteps of Jesus, The Christ. I thank You for once again revealing the true Principle to me. Wherein God is truly the All-in-All and I AM One with Him.

My love and thanksgiving.

Dear Child:
You have sought, prayed, desired; putting God Reality above all else. Follow The Christ path given to you. Rejoice and be exceedingly glad you have won a victory. Do not give in to defeat again. The Heavenly Host is with You.

#106 - Wednesday

Dear Precious Jesus Christ, My I AM Reality:
It really works! To see through the materialism and behold the One God. It gives a rapport with Reality resulting in calmness, peace, love, joy and energy. When I let my vision stop with the materialism out there, there is a barrier; a black mist behind which the light and presence of God Reality seems to be hidden. Oh, what a joy it is to be in tune with God. It brings wholeness. Even the thing on my nose is disappearing. I have been able to accomplish much and I have been sleeping well.

My great thanks and love to God Almighty.

Dearest Child:

The Banquet Table, with the Allness of God's Goodness is constantly spread before you. But unless you know that It is there, all is of no avail. There is a Principle to follow which you have discovered after much self-denial, dedication and prayer. But you must clear the way. Annihilate the materialistic barriers and behold, you are One with this Reality. This does not mean to isolate yourself from the material world, but rather, to know that it is but a passing shadow without credence and essence. Behold the God Essence. The only Reality. Be a seer, be free, be in the material world but not of it.

Go in peace.

#107 - Thursday

Dearest Guide, Parent, Teacher:

How I look forward to this time of communion each day. Never do I want to disregard nor to forget You. Would that I were more receptive to Your teachings for I know Your precepts are infinite. Too often I narrow the channel, because of personal concerns, anxieties, etc., through which You can express. That is why today I do not feel fully alive to Your divine energy, wholeness, beauty, harmony, peace. To be sure, since You express through Principle and Laws, You are unchanging, perfect, eternal; it is I who must align with You. Then all power, strength, Truth is shared... there are no limitations to infinity. Always Your teachings have so beautifully and easily unfolded in a way I know not of. But You, the Source, flows to me as streams from a mountain top. I know not what to expect, except to know You teach me in ways applicable to all. I have sought You with all my heart, for You are the essence, joy and fulfillment of my Being. Once more I listen. Speak!

With much gratitude and love.

Dearly Beloved Disciple:
You have asked and you have received. You have knocked and the door has been opened; there is no barrier between us. The glory of this Oneness is universal. There are no exceptions! I know how often you have felt I was slightly above your head looking on, helping, protecting. Often you ask Me to intercede and make known the Way of Truth. I have always heard; I have always responded. I AM your constant vigilance and advisor. I AM Your light, so how could there be anything unlike light which dissipates all darkness.

I express into visibility wherever there are no barriers; in a scientific procedure that is immutable. So you can trust Me and depend on Me. All around you can see signs of this. The grass turning green, the birds returning, the daffodils and tulips about to burst forth from their budding. These are sign posts, symbols of what is the essence behind and throughout.

My laws know no deviations. My Truths know no variance. My wholeness and wisdom know no segments. My light knows no darkness.

And you, the eternal you, have been made in My likeness. Awaken from your mortal sleep of duality! Awaken from your dreamlike stupor! Claim the Truth about yourself! Accept your divine heritage! Take the

easy way which lifts all burdens and makes you free, light and buoyant! Let Me be you, completely, wholly, beautifully! Dwell, abide in this true, Real Kingdom with Me! Away with shadows, untruths, mirages, forever! I have much more to share with you. By My grace you have been made whole, strong, wise, peaceful and loving.

Your eternal guide. Amen.

#108 - Saturday

Dearly Beloved God:
    You are ever active, ever powerful, ever present in my life. To see through the outer to You is the Principle of joy, elevation, peace, wholeness and beauty. To go back to the Source is a wonderful privilege and wise to the utmost. I go back to my true Source which was from the very beginning. This makes life so very simple and fruitful because then life is synchronized with God... the One Real Being. Too many words and definitions defer the arriving to this point of divine consciousness. Why make it complicated when it is so very simple, pure, whole, relaxing and uplifting. Glory to God and my great thanks for the revelation of this Truth. I love you.

My gratitude forever.

Dear Child:
    Purity in consciousness is essential. It must not be polluted with so called opposites of God. God is Essence, Spirit unconfined and so are you. Do not allow multiplicity to be a barrier to beholding the One God. Look

through the mist of mortality, for the mist is filled with mistakes, lies and delusions. Keep constant and One with God Reality. Keep the divine Principle always in your consciousness above everything else. Relax and be exceedingly glad that God is All and you are intrinsically One with this Allness. Life is meant to be beautiful, peaceful, joyous, easy and lovely.

Amen.

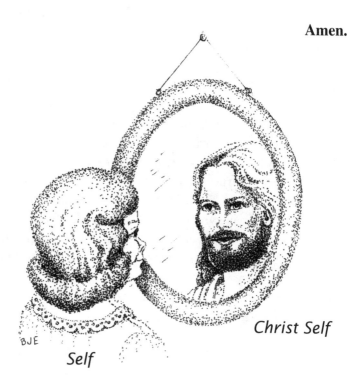

Christ Self

Self

How lovely does the world become
when you see the Truth
about yourself reflected back to you.

#109 - Sunday

Dear Wonderful God Reality:

I feel Oneness with Jesus Christ who gave us his beautiful Principle that so few understood. Even his disciples did not fully understand that there is only God Truth, in essence, in space, beneath the seas. Everywhere equally present, reverberating with life, vision, wisdom, joy, love and light; and the way to get through to this One Reality is to see through the sham of the outer to the I AM. This truly takes practice and I am beginning to see and accept the Truth and Reality of this Principle. Dear God, I thank You. Help me to always discipline myself to the One Truth and Reality.

My love and gratitude.

Dear Child:

You see the light having gone through shadows, mists in the outer and have arrived at the basic Truth. But it is up to you to always discipline yourself, moment by moment, day and night. All of God is with you to accept and glorify His Holy Name and presence. To try to tell this great Truth to others would be like trying to feed a baby steak. It would choke instead of swallowing it. This Truth is so tremendous and wonderful. It will be inspired in others by your example. Live It. Be It. Enjoy It. Glorify It and see this One Reality in all persons, places and things.

God is blessing you.

#110 - Tuesday

Dear Precious, Jesus Christ. My Love. My Reality:
     You have guided me through yesterday's busy day and helped me make many decisions. Without allowing the Principle to open the way to You, life would be restless, troublesome and perplexing. But by being One with You, the only Reality, life unfolds with a capital "L." Life abounding in joy, energy, enthusiasm, wholeness, light and love.

Love and thanks.

My Beloved Child:
     It would not be easy to feel in words how to reach this high plateau. Trying to explain the Principle would confuse most and few would accept it, but you must continue to live It, be It. Let others see your light and have their problems lightened. Keep on. The journey is beautiful and fulfilling.

God loves you.

#111 - Wednesday

Dearest Companion, Helper, Teacher, Guide:
     Once again, communion time is complete quiet. How peaceful and relaxing to be alone and yet All One with You. My heart overflows with gratitude for Your divine help. You have taught me not to feel the strain of labor because it is You that carries the load; much like recognizing that I do not feel wearied from the work performed by

electric appliances.

In a sense, You have worked through me much like electricity and I do not feel the weight of the job. How wonderful You are to me. Unfold more of Your spiritual Truths to me. I am ready and eager to live the Christ Way. May I have unfolded in such a way that You are pleased.

I love You and am grateful.

Dearly Beloved Child:

It has been said, "Many are called, but few are chosen." Please know that My call is to each and every one, but only a few have chosen Me. You have earnestly and sincerely sought Me; to receive more of My precepts, and I know of your gratitude and love. The worthy ones receive even more while little is taken away from those who do not have receptive hearts or do not desire to find me and become One with Me.

I know that this true Principle has confounded many, but I know that you have accepted this Principle. It is like a desert when no moisture falls on it; even the little moisture that may have been imbedded in the sand is dried up. You have called upon Me for Living-Waters so as not to experience the parched, desert-like barrenness. You have called upon Me to give, not as the world gives of materiality, which is here today and gone tomorrow (much like the leaves of spring are dried to nothingness in the fall), but you have asked for peace, harmony, wholeness, joy, wisdom, love... these are the essence of My Kingdom.

I rejoice in welcoming you into this Kingdom of Reality and sharing with you all I have. For all that I

have and AM is yours and you. There is great rejoicing here when even one from your realm reaches out in faith just a little. So much more of this wonderful Kingdom is yours to accept. So much more than you could possibly comprehend in the third dimension. But you have graduated. You have recently earned another diploma. Your attitude has improved; no more criticisms, complaints, condemnations. You no longer desire to be pitied for doing much, etc. Avoid any such feelings! Just be grateful! Any emotions that center on the little self are out of tune with Me. Enough for now. I will never leave you and will always pour more refreshing waters into your loving consciousness. I love you.

Amen.

#112 - Tuesday

Dear God. My Jesus Christ Reality:
Confession is good and I must relieve myself of the unhappiness caused by the interplay of individuals last night. I was hurt and I feel upset and blue. I feel like crying but I refrain from talking about my feelings. I don't want to indulge in negative feelings. Especially feelings of neglect and jealousy. Please show me the way to peace, relaxation and harmony my dear God.

My love and deep gratitude.

My Dearest Child:
Still growing up. You have allowed emotions to disturb you. Don't try to hold onto any individual.

146

Release. Let go even if it means a breaking up. Continue to see through the panorama of the physical world. Know that it passes and will be no more. Do not allow illusions to masquerade as Reality. Snap out of your doldrums and decide to be happy again.

#113 - Wednesday

Dearest Reality, My God, My Christ I AM:
   Last night I lay awake for hours contemplating my return to The Principle. The struggle, the searching goes on. Why is it that when I AM in tune with my Reality, all unfolds so beautifully and lovingly? And then I think this is so perfect and so easy. Why can't I help others to grasp this true Principle? Why do I then fall by the wayside and yearn so intensely to be One with Principle again? Refresh me. Reinstate me. Rejuvenate me.

                              I give my love and thanks.

Dearly Beloved:
   The mechanism of this Principle is so delicate and can be easily lost when identifying with the physical world. The least negative emotion can swerve one away from the straight and narrow path. Examine your emotions and you will discover that you have indulged in feelings of unhappiness, displeasure, suspecting, darkness and lack. It is not easy to dispel these emotions when they have grabbed you. These emotions are of the devil (ego)... so to speak. Immediately replace them with love, forgiveness, calming such emotions. These emotions will leave you and you will return to your radiant Christ Self,

shining, glowing and dispelling all gloom.

#114 - Friday

Dear Beloved Jesus Christ:

Yesterday I really hit bottom. I thought my "midnight of the soul" experiences were over for good; but how miserable and out of tune I feel. Yesterday evening I was almost at the point of tears. What has happened? I have been going along for so long riding the crest and now this slump. It seemed like I could do no right. Please rescue me from these depths of despair. Awaken me from this nightmare.

I thank You and love You.

Dear Child:

Your very desire to be awakened from these false episodes and three dimensional environment to find that you are already The Christ Self is the miracle, the joy. Do not feel sorry for your little self. This little, false self is the cause of all your frustrations and unhappiness. Transcend it. Rise above it and claim your divine heritage. Know who you are. Do not identify with your ego. It is not the Real you. Believe.

You are My precious child.

#115 - Monday

Dear Jesus Christ, the Angelic Host, My I AM Reality:

I am so very grateful for the help, guidance, peace

and joy that have come to me when I open the way to reach You, knowing always that You are there and awaiting my recognition and awareness of You. How joyous I am when we communicate and I feel Your abiding love. Sometimes there are feelings of upset and lack of love in my consciousness and so then I know that I have not made complete rapport with You. Never do I want to feel lost, upset or unhappy because of what goes on in the outer. Help me to be my own Christ Reality and not be moved by situations, conditions or people and their actions. Often I have reached this divine plateau and have abided One with You and have become my true spiritual Self for long periods of time. Like the prodigal, I yearn for renewal of this divine experience; to be reborn, to find my true Self and abide therein.

I thank You and love You supremely.

Dear Child:
Avoid feelings of self pity, neglect or any of the self attitudes even if your human self dictates such feelings. By accepting these negatives you are pushed down even lower. Rise above all earthly perceptions. Transcend the downward pull of gravity, of humanhood, of darkness and despair. Care not at all how you are treated. When claiming your Christ Reality, your feelings will be joyous, fulfilling, relaxing, glorious, true. Shift from the third dimension to the fourth dimension; from sense to soul.

Know that you are loved.

#116 - Wednesday

Dearest Christ, My Very Own I AM:
    Church has preceded this communion time. This was a fruitful period, but oh how much greater the inspiration and the divine outpouring when I am alone, One with You. I am so very grateful for Your divine touch and expression in my Beingness and crave even more from Your storehouse of wisdom (ideas), guidance, illumination, beauty, harmony, and wholeness.

                    I am receptive. Speak loving presence!

Dearly Beloved Child:
    You are growing up, learning to walk; so do not be downcast by falls and little hurts. Pick yourself up and "keep on keeping on!" You are Spirit in Truth and Your true habitation is that of Spirit, so infinite, perfect, beautiful, peaceful, joyous and what's more, It is Real, not fiction; It is the only Real abiding place. When fully awake, you will know that you are One with all this wonder and bliss.
    Live in this consciousness constantly and con- sciously. Awake to sleep no more... and behold what mortal eyes cannot see and realize. By grace you have spiritual vision. Ever keep thankful and at peace.

                    My blessings are infinite, Amen.

You are growing up, learning to walk;
so do not be downcast by falls and little hurts.
Pick yourself up and "keep on keeping on!"

#117 - Thursday

Dear Wonderful God Reality:

You are always awaiting my recognition and identi-fying with You as my own eternal Self . So it is up to me to make the contact; to let divine God Flow and live as me. When this Principle is followed, all unfolds easily and beautifully. There are so many activities coming up; travel plans and travel. It is very important to keep relaxed and be my Christ Self . If I allow myself to get involved with the outer too greatly, there is a downward pull (Satan), and uneasiness and upset follow. I must discipline little me and let my Christ Self take over and reign.

My love and gratitude.

My Dearest Child:

There are really not two of you. The Christ you and the mortal you. There is only One. Your Christ Reality. For nothing is truly Real that changes. If you can see it, it is not forever. You are The Christ Reality. Your one and only true Self. The mortal you sees only shadows, illusions, temporal, ephemeral. Only the divine substance; the essence that is everywhere equally present and unchanging is Real. Make life easy without burdens or concerns. Be not anxious about unrealities. Laugh off the ridiculous.

#118 - Friday

Dear Precious, All Present and All Powerful God:

To find You and my Oneness with You has been my

goal and the greatest achievement possible. I know You have been seeking me even more than I You. The days when I identify with my eternal, spiritual Self; relaxed on the stream of God's life and essence; all unfolds well. Then what do I say when disturbances with the outer try to obliterate my Oneness with God? I say, "I know the Truth; God is All and all else is unreal, illusions and passing shadows." Some call the attempted disorder the devil or Satan. But I know from the time I have forgotten who I really AM; so an entrance was made from non-reality to come in. I must stay firm in the Truth.

My love and gratitude.

Dear Child:
Knowing the Truth about your Reality is not enough. You must be this relaxed, spiritual Self always and let It be you and live for you. Do not forget to claim your divine inheritance, otherwise you live a lie. Always be aware of God Reality and your Oneness with the All. Then the entire Kingdom of God; the Realm of Reality is open to you to serve you; to solve your problems; to lead you and make whole. Isn't this wonderful? Rejoice and be exceedingly glad always.

I love you.

#119 - Wednesday

Dear Jesus Christ, My Guide, Healer and Helper:
I come to You praying for a physical healing. Perhaps I have strayed away from the Principle, the Formula

that God is the only Reality. All else is illusion. God is unchanging, eternal. All in the outer comes and goes. Dear Jesus, take my hand and lead me into the Truth that dissipates all lies. Lead me out of this tunnel to the divine light wherein my consciousness is illuminated so that it blends One with God's Allness. I seek, I search, I ask, and now I welcome acceptance.

Love and gratitude.

Dear Child:

Your Real eternal Self, spiritual Self, is the one and only you. It is your own Reality. The never changing, perfect Reality you are searching for. Accept and be this One. Often you have found It, but you must continually live It. Radiating out of It and letting go of all concerns in the physical world. Never be disturbed by appearances that want your attention. These are the devils and deserve no consideration for Satan is the opposite of God and since God has no opposites, they are nothing.

Amen.

#120 - Sunday

Dearly Beloved Christ of My Being:

I love and appreciate this communication time... so peaceful, unhurried, joyous! Today is Independence Day. Speak to me of freedom, bondage. I invite this illumination. May I unfold into greater spiritual understanding.

My gratitude and love.

154

Dearly Beloved Child:

To illumine you concerning freedom and the so-called opposite, bondage, I must, as always, adhere to the divine Principle. True freedom can only be realized, lived and expressed when one has awakened to his true Being. One can only be totally free when he is aware of its true identity, which always has been, in Reality, and always will be.

Free from what? Free from all the so-called opposites of God. When one has accepted the Truth that $2 \times 2 = 4$, he is automatically free from all the other so-called equations, numerous as they could be, that are untrue lies, and which can only result in the wrong answer... anxieties, unsolved problems, frustrations, etc.

Each one, as a child of God, is right now completely and wholly Spiritually Free. But how few know, realize, identify with It. This is one's glorious heritage... complete freedom in living as One with God... his prisoner. This sounds like a paradox, but It is so beautiful and wonderful when understood. When wandering away in consciousness from this Kingdom of Reality, one forfeits his freedom like the prodigal son, until he returns (in consciousness) to His Father's Home. Until then, what chains one puts upon himself; what bondage he succumbs to... a slave to what you call sin, materiality, falsities, lies that seem to him so real and authentic!

What a price to pay for forfeiting, giving up the only Freedom there is... one's glorious unity with the Father!! But all the while that one feels himself imprisoned, impoverished, sinful, unhappy, sick, the prison doors are locked. He can open them and walk out at any time, when he "comes to Himself" and awakens to His

Christ Self and knows who he really is; and that in the Father's arms, he can be safe, secure, whole, forever and ever. His soul is set free when he desires to be a prisoner of God, which has always been his true habitation.

One can, in Truth, be free regardless of outer circumstances and conditions. The very attitude of being free in Spirit, One with God, in His love, life and Truth, automatically changes the outer picture. Once again, this is so simple and childlike. It is the message that Jesus The Christ had in His heart to convey to others. It is still so true and the only Truth. All else is bondage. Be free! Be joyous! Be whole! Be The Christ Self, now and forever... One with Me.

Amen.

#121 - Tuesday

Dearly Beloved Jesus Christ. My Savior, My Helper:

Thank You for being with me every moment yesterday. It was a very busy day but all unfolded so joyfully, easily and beautifully. The next three weeks will continue to be very busy. I must abide close to You keeping afloat on your Everlasting Arms feeling our Oneness.

I thank You and love You. Shine through me.

Dearest Child:

Relax and live each moment as it comes. Believe that it brings its own fulfillment and completeness. Never feel anxious, worried or concerned. All that is going on in the outer eventually passes away like shadows. Try to make every occasion a happy one knowing that God is the only presence and power. Pass these tasks with flying colors. You are prepared. Relax! Enjoy! Be at peace for you have come to awaken others to their Christ Reality.

#122 - Thursday

Dear Wonderful God Reality:

How important it is for me to have this sacred communication time with You. Too often the "counterfeit" world tries to push its way into my consciousness with all its false ideas, glamour, activities. But I must keep myself in balance with You at the hub of All. I know, God, You are the eternal, unchanging One and are the only activity, substance, presence. It is good to review the Truth often so that the falseness of the world does not encroach upon me. Help me to keep my spiritual balance so that I know I AM a spiritual Being.

My love and gratitude to you.

Dear Child:
You are in rhythm with Reality. But remember that you can enjoy the beauty of the rose even while knowing its time is brief; for it too will fade and fall away. Always look through the symbol to behold the One God and you will enjoy the pictures of humanhood even more because you know "it has come to pass." Rely only on God Reality which never fails or forsakes. The secret is to let the outer pass and fill your concerns with

glories of God that ever grow, brighten and become more radiant.

God loves you.

#123 - Saturday

Dearly Beloved Jesus Christ.

You taught us the Truth about man's relation to Him, but so few have believed; having faith in only what they can see, feel, touch, hear. They believe in the senses thus believing in the material world and that man is the only reality. Jesus taught just the opposite; that these temporal seemings must be transcended to behold the One Reality, the One God, the only presence, power, intelligence. I must have grasped this eternal Truth more clearly yesterday because I felt the joy, the presence; almost the push of God Reality to live through me. I thank You for coming through and how I lived yesterday I pray may continue always.

My love and gratitude to Jesus Christ, to God.

Dear Child:

You have become an "over comer." To be sure, you have had mountains to climb which strengthened your spiritual leap. You have sought, searched for, prayed to find the true Reality of God's never changing, ever present, light (ideas), love, life. This treasure of Truth must be earned and cannot be bought in a store as a gift. Jesus said, "This is the way." You walk in It, believe It, rejoice in It and give thanks for It. The price must be paid by each searcher.

#124 - Thursday

Dearest Divine Christ, My True Self:

Dear Father, when I know that You, and You alone
are my true Self, why do I fall away from this Truth and
waddle around in the false, in which unhappiness, frustration, illness put me in bondage? I want no more to be in the
clutches of such false powers. I know that when I return to
You, (like the prodigal); when I awaken from spasmodic
nightmares, when I completely tune into Your Reality and
feel our Oneness, I am immediately released from all the
negations in the horrible apartness. And so the physical
ailment (sore throat) that recently seemed to cause trouble,
was immediately dissipated and disappeared into its nothingness when I arose in consciousness and claimed my true
identity, The Christ, forever Your prisoner. Would that I
always live in the consciousness of Your glory and eternal
love and perfect infinity. Your grace has made me whole.
May I always choose You as the only Reality, only presence,
only activity.

My love and gratitude.

Dearly Beloved Child:
**... who wavers so frequently like a pendulum,
from the Father's Allness, to the shadows of despair and
unhappiness!**
**The fruits of the Spirit are My eternal gift to you.
The Christ is each one's true Reality as Jesus exemplified. Forever and now, I stay closer to you than breathing to answer your requests, to welcome you to the fold,
to instruct, guide, teach. There is great delicacy and**

precision required, complete dedication to the Truth, as well as complete surrender and letting go all the limitations, shadows, unrealities, in order to abide constantly in the Kingdom of Heaven. Do not be tempted to forfeit the peace, the joy, the perfection, the wisdom that is truly thine as My child! (The Christ!). Discipline the little self that so easily gets ensnared by things of the world, that result in worry, anxieties, fears... these conspire to throw one off balance and off base.

Keep your consciousness pure. Be strong in your convictions of Truth and Truth Principles. See through the outer play of shadows and behold the One Reality, the substance of All. In God, there is nothing to fear. Perfect answers, divine help are always forthcoming. Keep poised, joyous, wise.

#125 - Saturday

Dear Precious Jesus:

You lived as The Christ and showed us the way to find our Christ. These talks mean so much to me. To commune and to tune in to the Realm of Reality; to have a Principle to live by. I am so grateful and love You supremely. When I stay in tune with You, I feel Your guidance. God, You are All; filling all space and besides You, there is nothing else but fiction, fables, illusions and passing drama.

My great love to You.

My Dear Child:
Attunement, alignment, rapport works both ways. With you, with Me there is no cutting off. Only a

continuous flow of life on which you are privileged to rest. Let go of all false claims so that you can let the God power flow. It is all so simple. Never allow complications to enter in. Do not adulterate the simplicity of the Truth with complexities and needless words. Just live It. Be It. Radiate It. Rejoice and be exceedingly glad.

Amen.

#126 - Monday

Dear Precious Jesus Christ:

Although we gave a nice party at the Inn, I wasn't in tune with You. I felt uncomfortable, ill at ease, awkward and last night's sleep was not restful. I pray to keep in constant flow with You.

My love and gratitude.

My Dear Child:

I know you are trying, but too often you allow things in the world to overtake you. Yet you have grasped Truth that everything comes to pass. They appear to disappear. Also, you cannot live in the tomorrow until they are the now, today. Do not care what others think, say or do. Wash clean your plate of "otherness" so that there is a clean and open channel for your Christ I AM to express. Know that this "I AM" is your Real and only Reality. You cannot remember the concerns and upsets of the past 5, 10, 20 years. But you do remember that you were seeking your Christ Reality and a Truth Principle that you could apply constantly.

Keep on disciplining yourself and dedicating yourself to the One God Reality. Know that all is well, NOW! Relax, rejoice and be exceedingly glad.

I AM with you, always.

#127 - Tuesday

Dearest Divine Presence. My Very Own Father-Mother:
How glorious to feel that I AM truly Your child. My heritage is so perfect and wonderful. It is my desire to look unto You for all my help, guidance and security; much as a little child regards his earthly parents. I want so much to relinquish the personal, (for "persona" is the mask that conceals Your Reality, the eternal Kingdom of Heaven, harmony, joy and perfection).

May I realize now that I already abide in this Kingdom and that all else is like pictures on a screen that eventually pass and disappear. I AM the light since I AM Your child. I know that the pictures that are presenting themselves, both beautiful, and not so lovely, harmonious and not so perfect, are doomed to eventually passing away. And yet I still seek Your perpetual help, guidance, reassurance, illumination.

Thank you, divine parent.

Dear Child of Mine:
I love you even more wholly and purely than any earthly parent could possibly love his child. It is My desire to help you and set all things aright and in divine order; so fall in rhythm with Me. I know you perceive

the light, My presence, as I envelop you this morning in the kitchen. It's glorious for Me to know that I AM identified, accepted, praised, in all humility and joy.

To be sure, you seem to have many problems in a family, in a social way. But know that already All is done, All is well, All is finished, All is perfect. The "pattern" is complete. Just ask to perceive It, and be willing to accept It even though It is not in accordance with what you may have desired. I AM your guidance, Your light, Your overall discerner.

Believe in Me. Take it easy. Relax! Be joyous, full of the Spirit of the divine. Let Me express through you, My child. You be My mouthpiece. How wonderful that you have ascended from the material, where to the mortal, all this seems to be Real. But you have transcended to the invisible, perfect, Realm of Truth. You have become spiritually strong in order to be thus "promoted." I have faith in you.

Amen.

#128 - Friday

Dear Wonderful Reality, God:

During a restless, sleepless night (seemingly starting up a cold), and worrying how things would unfold when Amy is here next week; the presence of my father revealed himself as his spiritually perfect, young, handsome Self. He came to me so vividly with the thought that if I would identify and coincide with him, all would immediately be transformed from sense to soul, One with and like my father's. What peace, joy and wholeness followed. Some-

163

thing is trying to break through and reveal a new plateau to me during my "midnight of the soul" experiences. My father's spiritual Self and my identity are One with It. Always receiving guidance, wholeness, wisdom, peace and glory. Now I have his Reality to keep ever alive in my consciousness.

My great love and appreciation.

Dear Child:
When you think you are in the "midnight experience," it is only a cleansing to make way for a new and higher dimension. Your father's presence has always been with you, but now you have awakened to the Truth that he never left you. He is the link that connects and opens the entire Kingdom of Reality for you. Cling to this Heavenly link and give it the praise and the thanks for wholeness, joy, peace, energy.

I love you.

#129 - Monday

Dear Precious Father, My Jesus Christ Presence:
Thank You for Your presence and guidance while my eight year old granddaughter Amy was with us. I seemed to float along on Your divine current and all unfolded easily, joyfully, harmoniously. Even at Amy's young age she is aware of Your presence, power and love. How gloriously her life will unfold. And now there are many pieces to fit into our schedule (travel, entertaining, cleaning). You are always with me to give guidance and illumination.

Dear Child:
You felt whole and happy because you were serving a purpose and you kept joyous and light. Unless you become as a little child, you cannot enter the Kingdom of God. You can learn from a child as you did from Amy. Worry not. Fear not. All the pieces of your puzzle will fit into your schedule perfectly. Keep afloat. Do not allow concerns of anything in the physical world to pull you down to the level of humanhood. Be peaceful, kind, loving and joyful.

I AM with you always.

#130 - Tuesday

Dearest Angel of My Presence:
You have helped me through a weekend of baby sitting with my grandson. I confess that the apprehensions and anxieties beforehand far exceeded the actual unfolding. I thank You for giving me the insight to keep calm, quiet, loving. All went well, and once again I feel that I have taken a test and passed.

This morning upon awakening, I had a feeling of being One, in fact, an integral part of all infinity. I felt absorbed in Your perfect peace, harmony, wholeness, joy... as if I were behind scenes in the actual All unchanging cause and fount of All and looking on the outer... being wiser, seeing All in the visible as a moving, shifting, changing scene, and my mortal body in this same ephemeral picture.

If this is my reward, what a wonderful gift, to have the true consciousness to perceive All as It really is in Truth, through the eyes of Christ Self. I thank You and it is my prayer that It remains with me.

Love and thanks.

Dearly Beloved Radiance of My Angelic Presence:
All Reality glows with love when even one soul
has grasped the Truth of Being. You have been preparing in the school of difficult lessons, to learn, and with
passing grades, to awaken, to receive, to accept, this most
wonderful gift, reward, diploma, that could possibly be
given to a child of your Father-Mother God. You have
asked, searched, and readied your soul for this grasping
and realizing of Holy Oneness, which is ecstasy, joy,
completeness, wholeness, glory! It is yours to keep forever, as long as you keep centered and aware of the
realm of realization and feel your melting of Oneness in
the Holy of Holies.
In this way, God's good flows to you unceasingly.
Your tasks are unburdened and become delightful activities. You know your health is My health, wholeness...
where nothing could be out of place, imperfect.
You have learned that existing as a little separate
being within your own world (false as it is) of physical
boundaries and identifications is horrible, which,
through ignorance of the Truth, you had brought on
yourself. The price for this ignorance, this lack of
perceiving what is true and not true, what is Real and
not real, is so very great that darkness (instead of light,
My light) seemed to be everywhere. You have earnestly
sought Me and My grace has admitted you into My
Heaven of cause where all is perfect, unchanging...
abounding in divine ideas and Truths!

Keep awake to this wonderful wonder. I will always be by your side, so to speak, and more and more and more will flow into your awareness (consciousness). Because you have chosen Me, I have chosen you to be My channel to express and radiate through to the "world of shadow," to bring light to the "not-knowing," and thus to awaken them from their mortal nightmares of illusive dream.

I love you!

#131 - Saturday

Dear God, One Presence, One Reality:
     The last few days there has been searching and seeking to find the divine pattern or Principle with which to live and breathe and find perfection of body, harmony, joy and wisdom. So often I have lived in Your divine dimension of Reality and experienced joy, peace, love, harmony and so there are feelings of being lost when not living in tune with You in the presence of Jesus, The Christ. My Christ Self yearns to be recognized and live through me. There have been things in the outer that have bothered me and must be overcome. Help me to be my eternal Reality, unchanging, perfect. My true eternal body of God is ever present, joyous, perfect, whole, complete. Let there be even more rapport and divine wisdom! My love to the One, All-to-gether, lovely and Almighty.

My Dear Child:
     Seeking and finding, what could be more important than to make the journey from sense to soul? To

know your own eternal Christ Self , and to know that all elseness only comes to pass, is temporal and only appearances. **I AM with you always to uplift, strengthen, guide and give you peace, joy, perfection, wisdom. Look through the maze, shadows and behold the One God.**

#132 - Wednesday

Dear Ever Constant Presence, Power, Love, Joy:
   Monday and Tuesday unfolded well. Had vitality, peace of mind, and slept well Monday evening. But not so last night. Help me to get back in tune with You again! To accomplish much, yes feel relaxed-being The Temple and regarding all else as shadows, appearing, changing, then disappearing. My real concern is my prayer to become perfect! Clarify my thinking and feeling. Take over for me so that Your life is my life, Your perfection is my wholeness. Dear Jesus, who lived as I want to live, and to become The Christ, here and now. Give me light, joy, perfection, eliminating all the shadows of nothingness. You are My guide, way shower, healer, and to You my...

Love and gratitude.

My Special Child:
   Special because you have earnestly sought My presence and guidance. Your prayers are heard and fulfilled. Feel light! Full of light, love, life. Relax. Have no regrets nor worries. The Real you is perfect, whole, complete. Your I AM, One with Me, and I could have no imperfections, fears... only wholeness, completeness, love, joy, peace. Awaken to Reality. Do not allow shadows to cast

darkness and upsets. They are nothing and soon disappear. You have All in All. Rejoice!

Blessings, love, Amen.

#133 - Thursday

Dearest Father-Mother God, My Own Christ:
    This is my happy time again, when I really feel that we are in rapport, in open communication, and with great love. My fervent desire is to share this wonderful experience and privilege, for You are the pearl beyond price. How I wish I could awaken others who are grabbing crumbs that cannot satisfy, when the banquet table is so elegantly, lovingly, beautifully and fulfillingly spread before them. To open their Spiritual Eyes so that they can behold the Kingdom of Heaven, here and now, would give me such a wonderful feeling of not having lived in vain. Dearly beloved partner, guide me, enlighten me, open my Spiritual Eyes more and more. My love and gratitude to You is immeasurable.

Dearly Beloved Co-Partner:
    Remember years ago when I gave you the vision that changed your entire life? You had been prayerfully seeking, otherwise you could not have received this great illumination. Also, during your life, you have repeatedly applied the Principle that was given to you in this divine vision. I know you can still see this emaciated man with arms stretched up and eyes looking Heavenward pleading with God to be merciful and supply food lest he starve. And all the while there was a long banquet table,

with all kinds of delicious and attractive foods, spread elegantly before him.

Although God's provision is abundant and right at hand, it does no good unless one opens his eyes and beholds the feast spread before him and partakes of It. God's work is already done. It is complete, perfect, wonderful! But man, immersed in humanhood with all the veils of materiality and the personal self pulled down, hiding and concealing the Great Feast, seems often to be content with his misery, lacks, disappointments, troubles, and does not even desire to awaken. He wants to continue in his old rut, never taking time to commune with God, the only Reality with whom he is truly One. He would rather dwell in the shadows of TV, radio, newspapers, novels, social life, etc. These are certainly not the Source of true happiness, nor the avenues leading to The Christ Self .

As zealous as you are to help others to awaken and to enjoy the "Fruits of the Spirit" as you have, the initial step must be an inner one on their part. You cannot eat for another's nutrition. You cannot carry water back from the river unless you have a container, which must be empty and without leaks. And the larger and more perfect the container, the more water it can hold.

This is Principle as is all of God's teachings. Principles that are immutable, perfect, indestructible, glorious! But these Principles are more than cold, indifferent laws... they are intimately related to each individual, though undivided in the whole.

*Although God's provisions are abundant and
right at hand, it does no good unless one opens
his eyes and beholds the feast spread before him
and partakes of it.*

Dearly Beloved One, keep on keeping in rapport with Me letting Me flow through you and live through you. Do not be overly concerned with those who are indifferent or disinterested in the Spiritual Banquet spread before them. Just behold The Christ, the Reality in each and let go of anxieties. By My grace you have been given these redeeming Truths. Live them. Be them. Be free, joyous, radiant!

Love, divine blessings overflowing, Amen.

#134 - Friday

Communion Time With My Own Christ I AM:
One with the All present, All power, All love, Reality. Almost continually there have been desires and attempts by me to find and be the "Temple not made with hands." Eternal in the Realm of Reality (Heaven). The more this divine essence, Reality, love is felt, the more easily and perfectly my day unfolds. Always there is a desire and prayer to have even a clearer comprehension and feeling of God's presence and Reality, to take over for me and be me, to be present in the ever active, perfect, wonderful Kingdom of God here and now, a desire for a more fervent, clear and alive at-one-ment. My great thanks and love for helping me along the way.

My love and adoration.

My Dear Seeker and Finder, My Eternal Child:
The more you release your hold on material, which is like a veil, a barrier, a cloud, a shadow, the

more clear and alive is your perception and feeling that God is All. Ever present and active, filling All space, time with the ecstasy of His (My) Spirit. You have succeeded greatly in transcending the transparency. Keep on in a relaxed and joyful atmosphere, abiding in the Temple, the Kingdom of God and releasing your hold on all else.

Amen.

#135 - Monday

Dearest Divine Presence, My Very Own Angel, Guardian:
    Our relationship grows ever more serene, beautiful, meaningful, real, as this communion time continues. This presence of Thine I recognize ever more constantly, and rely on It for guidance, help, security, wholeness, joy.

Gratitude fills my consciousness.

Dearly Beloved Object of My Affection:
    I could feel your very high vibration this morning and that true joy and well being permeated your consciousness. Getting through to you more constantly is like a rivulet going over the same area time and time again until a crevice is formed, then a ditch, then a valley, a chasm, and a canyon. Deeper and deeper is our relationship and this is glorious for both of us.
    I have welcomed you to look behind the scenes and find Me, to look beyond the facade of the materialist's drama and to see the cause, to find the Source, your own indwelling Christ, your I AM. The outer scene now in the springtime is filled with beauty,

loveliness, fragrance, delight. But all this is but an act, to tell of the wonders behind the scene. God is the author of this "play" and although the "play" gives hints about the author, do not mistake the "play" as being the author. It is His product, much like a painting is not the artist himself! Get this clear, so as to avoid pitfalls that result from misidentification.

Take things as they come but always translating into the language of the eternal God. There are no secrets when at last you have found Me. The Book of Life is open and I gladly share the eternal Truths for hearts waiting expectantly like yours.

My love is infinite and unchanging, Amen.

#136 - Tuesday

Dear Ever Present Guide, Healer, Power, God:
Often Your divine instruction is with me upon awakening in the mornings. Then half asleep it is pondered in my heart and is a Truth to accept and live by. This morning recalls a book "Try Giving Yourself Away,"(I gave a book report on it, years ago). So this morning, the divine guidance was with me to try giving myself, my body, my All, into the hands of God, ever near and sweetly powerful. And so it is a way to release my hold on the physical body and all cares and anxieties and surrender to the eternal ethers. Years ago I wrote an article titled, "All of Me is All of God" and this substantiates what the divine guidance was giving me this morning. And so I have been applying this Principle and the result is relaxation, wholeness, perfection, peace, joy, light, guidance, harmony. Thus letting God be me and take over

for me.

My gratitude and love forever.

My Dear Child:
Your prayer for wholeness, perfection, light, guidance was unfolded to you this morning when you were relaxed and receptive. Keep this Principle ever One in your consciousness and practice. It is the best union with God; it is the Way, Truth and Life. To relinquish all to the One and Only Divine Being, putting all your cares and responsibilities on the One presence, power, thus melting into His Oneness, this is a great blessing.

#137 - Tuesday

Dear Divine Presence:
The One All powerful, loving, whole, complete. My prayer is to straighten me out, help me to get back in harmony with You. Slept not well last night. Too many concerns "out there." Fill my consciousness with the eternal Truth, my spiritual, eternal Self. Take my hand and lead me to the eternal Truth. Why should there be feelings of being lost? Anchor me to Your true eternal Reality. I listen. Instruct!

I love You above all else.

My Dear Child:
Nothing has changed in the Kingdom of God, the Realm of Reality, wherein your eternal Self abides. Right now you are a spiritual Being, complete, perfect, ever One with God Reality. And so you are perfect,

whole, complete, as joyous and pure as God Reality. Do not confuse shadows with Reality. All out there in the world appears to be Real, eternal, but those are only appearances (like on a TV screen). Look through and behold the unchanging One. Your consciousness is your Reality. Relax in the Everlasting Arms and be at peace.

#138 - Thursday

Dear Divine, Eternal Presence, My God, Unchanging:
    First, my thanks for Your guidance, substance, wholeness while traveling from Florida. All went well. My prayer is to so completely identify with, and to claim my eternal perfection so that there shall be an awakening from three dimensional illusions. Wherein, I have concerns to claim my eternal perfection as Your child, being One with You. Open my spiritual eyes so as to behold Your wonderful Oneness, perfection, light, glory, joy. I thank You for hearing my plea, knowing You are instantly present, active, redeeming! My nights' rest has been very good, for which I am thankful. Dear God, my invitation to be my, I AM and live in, through, and for me. In less than a second You are instantly everywhere radiating Your wisdom, power, perfection, love.

My gratitude and love

Dear Child:
    Sometimes you seem to be on the fence between sense and soul. You must completely relinquish the temporal, passing, untrue shadows of the outer and accept and immerse your thinking, feeling soul to be

your eternal, spiritual Self. The Real, eternal, perfect, unchanging Self , from sense to soul. I AM with you always, perfection, wholeness, never changes. Oneness can not be divided. Wholeness equals Allness, One to One. Accept and Be! I AM with you always, constantly, instantly, whole, perfectly, joyfully, wisely, beautifully.

#139 - Monday

Dearest Angel, My Christ:

Our exclusive time together for me (little me) to unload my problems, perplexities, anxieties, and for You (my I AM Christ) to supply the answers, the soothing balm, the immortal Truths and Principles. I am so very grateful for this rapport and so greatly do I desire to have a clear channel so that more of You can pour through.

My rest last night was not peaceful and relaxing as usual. Such a parade of thoughts this little mortal mind was staging. I wanted so much to stop this silly procession but somehow I had difficulty tuning in with You. Is this the result of my recent getting out of tune?

The way is certainly narrow and straight but I want this to be my journey. I want life to express through me easily, joyfully, fulfillingly.

My thanks!

Dearly Beloved "Ongoer:"
Yes, whenever one strays (in feelings, attitudes, from Christ attunement) into the byways, overgrown with thorns and thistles; there seems to be uncomfortable entanglements, hurts and anxieties, frustrations,

much as a little child experiences when lost in a crowd, temporarily separated from his parents.

Do not wander! Do not engage in hurt feelings, negative emotions, thus giving the devil (the ego, opposite of what I AM) a chance to grab you when you are off guard. Graduate from ignorance to wisdom. That is what this Truth is all about. You are made in God's image and likeness and when you thus identify with your true Self, life is beautiful, easy, joyous, fulfilling! You have free will and you make the choice. Most of your journeying has been on the straight and narrow; that is why you feel even more frustrated and unhappy when you detour and get lost.

I AM Spirit, as you are. We are One. Just invite Me to live each day for you, speak through you, act through you, shine through you, to awaken others from their mortal drowsiness. This is My desire, to have a pure, unadulterated, loving channel to radiate out from. You have desired Me, longed for Me, loved Me, had faith in Me, to do just that. Together there is harmony and agreement. We are necessary to each other on earth, on your level of expression as in Heaven. Remember Oneness.

Love and blessings, Amen.

#140 - Tuesday

Dearly Beloved Reality:

How I searched to feel Your presence during the night. Awake from 3 a.m. on, and praying all the time. I need a clear comprehension of Your Reality and my Oneness with

You. Come through to me. Erase all the negatives, errors, frustrations, worries! I want and need only You. Clarify the debris in my thinking. My prayer is for wholeness, wisdom, joy, light, love and to see through the illusion of materiality. This pinnacle of consciousness has been reached before. Help me to unfold into this clear, eternal, beautiful, whole realization.

I thank You and love You.

My Dear Child:
The Journey from sense to soul is not always easy, especially when allowing persons, circumstances, places to invade your thinking, feeling, your consciousness! It is a straight and narrow way. But the way in which Jesus walked, he had times when getting away alone (All, One with God) was necessary. He knew the fiction of the outer, materiality, but so often lies, errors tried devilishly to rob Him of His divine peace, light, wisdom, as God's heir and Way Shower. Let go all seeming distraction and feel God's presence surrounding you!

I love you.

#141 - Wednesday

Dear One Reality, One Presence, One Essence:
I have found my Reality melted into Your Oneness. This is glorious, the answer, to be One with the All, which minimizes or obliterates, or crosses out all the intricacies of the outer which are passing, unreal. To see through the

sham to my I AM, One with God, in His flow and activity is the divine answer. The many items of activities that are stacked up in the future, are placed in God's care and Reality to be filled with His presence and wisdom and guidance and activity. My God, I AM One with Jesus Christ.

My great love and gratitude.

My Dear Child:
You have chosen Me to guide and illuminate your life. This has been your desire from childhood and now in your adult years the Truth about God Reality is ever present and active in your livingness. You can depend on God's presence, divine activity to lead you, guide you, live through and for you. Do not allow negativity in the outer (person, place, thing) to take control over you. Say "no" to these imposters; see them as nothingness, with no reality or power to divert you from your Christ Center. Be adamant. Keep still, poised and close to Christ presence and so rejoice that you are the Master, the winner, the peace maker!   All is well... always and in Truth, when you abide by God's teachings.

Be a good student!

#142 - Monday

Dearly Beloved Divine Presence:
Yesterday was a day of need, of perfection, of healing, of searching, seeking, praying. Oh, how I desired to feel Your abiding presence. Upon awakening early this morning, I dedicated the time to feeling Your divine pres-

ence, through me, and enveloping and encircling me. I could feel Your power, active, glowing, permeating all of me. I could feel Your mind... Your divine essence filling my consciousness! This presence, this power, this wisdom, this One God, so actively with me, so light, so pure, so whole and beautiful that I want to have this presence remain with me... so actively alive, so permeating, so fulfilling, so glorious.

This divine presence, this One God can always be my answered experience. Help me be aware of this unfailing, active, presence... my eternal Christ Self ... One with God. I pledge and endeavor to feel, to recognize this wonderful presence, always permeating my Being, always with me, always living for me and fulfilling all needs, lighting my way, speaking in and through me... thus eliminating all else, all the outer with its concerns, worries, upsets. This is the glorious Easter message, the living, active, power and presence always enveloping me.

My love and gratitude.

Dear Child:
    This is the answer for which you have been seeking and praying. You are filled with the One presence and power... God. But you must recognize It, feel It, be aware always of such permeating, gloriously active presence, power, wisdom... your true and eternal body. So let go all falseness, all outer barriers, all worries and concerns of the world. Live as One with the One presence and power, glorifying and exulting in this One wonderful, all fulfilling presence... God! This should be your only goal (reason for living)... all else vanishes and

is no more. **Rely, consult, feel, thank this abiding presence, encircling you, lighting and enlightening your
way... the ALL. Let go all else... God is All and is One
with You.**

God loves you.

#143 - Tuesday

Dearest Guardian Angel:

Sorry to have allowed my consciousness to drop to a
low level yesterday. For in humanhood I felt unloved,
unappreciated, neglected. To be sure, these very feelings are
signals, warning signs that I have wandered away in consciousness from Your presence, so that it was impossible to
be in rapport and to allow Your wonderful teaching and
blessings to come through. I guess I was being something
like a mathematician who thought he knew the formulas, the
multiplication tables, etc. Then in moments of forgetting or
ignorance, used these principles incorrectly and so came up
with the wrong answer. I certainly came up with the wrong
answer yesterday. I felt as miserable and perplexed as such a
mathematician would feel in similar circumstances.

All this shows I have much yet to learn and to do and
must apply these Principles even more carefully and
consistently. Pitfalls are just off the straight and narrow path
so I must walk in illumination and by Your grace.

My love and gratitude.

**Dearly Beloved Child of Mine:
You are forgiven as quickly and completely for**

your mistakes as a wise mother forgives her child for his
erroneous ways... always assuring the little one that she
still, and will always love him, but to let him know that
she does not agree with his mistakes in behavior, etc.
And so with you, do not hold yourself in condemnation,
nor criticize severely. Let go of these erroneous thoughts
and then the unhappy feelings that result from these will
disappear.

When you are identifying yourself with your own
Reality, the very Christ of you, of course you will be
loved and adored. It is only when you fall away from this
feeling of Oneness with Me that you feel separate, apart
and lonely. Then this little shadow self begins to indulge
in self-pity and even wants self-glorification and to feel
self-righteous.

Don't you see how this wrong identification is a
trap to catch you and bind you and make you a prisoner? When you are really glorifying The Christ Self
and feeling your Oneness with divine love, harmony,
peace, goodness, perfection, what should it matter to you
if those humans on the material plane do not regard you
lovingly? Already you are abiding in All the true and
Real love that there is in the entire universe. And then it
seems as a strange paradox that when you have released
all concern about human love, no longer desire it,
or even care, then it flows to you easily, naturally,
beautifully.

All this is so simple. Do not complicate it by
allowing the little self to intrude and assert its false
claims. Be free from such bondage. Exult in the Father's
love that never ceases, changes, diminishes! Be wise! Do
not be willing to pay a tremendous price for falling away

from the Truths I have so lovingly given you. All negative feelings are washed away and you, My child are as clean as the fresh fallen snow.

Amen.

#144 - Thursday

Dearest Super-Conscious, My Divine Co-Partner:

You have not departed from me. That, I know is impossible. But somehow yesterday I strayed and was lost in a wilderness of frustrations, upsets, discomfort, awkwardness. At the wedding reception it seemed that I felt so out of place, said things that should have been left unsaid, and neglected to say and do things that I should have said and done. Help me, divine redeemer, to get back in tune with You, to feel at ease, relaxed, peaceful and joyful. It is so unlike Heaven to be caught in a web of distortion and frustration. Free me from such bondage. No longer, do I want to be a prisoner to humanhood... only Your eternal prisoner. And from Your divine love, grace and harmony, may I never more escape. Help me forever and ever.

I love You.

Dearly Beloved "Wanderer:"

You may have seemed lost, but all the while, you were safe, secure, and fulfilled in My keeping. Deviation from Principle, from being aware of our Oneness, demands a toll. It is through such suffering as you experienced yesterday that you sincerely yearn to return to your Father's home and once more realize your security, peace and abundance. It is only when you feel apart, when you wandered in consciousness to believing your-self to be a human, a mortal, that you feel cast out from the Kingdom of Heaven. It is this personal sense that leads to frustrations and anxieties. It is the block that seems to shut out the Holy of Holies. Transcend your thoughts and feelings from that of a person of such and such height, weight, coloring, dress, etc., and identify with your true Self, The Christ. Let go the false person... take the attitude... I couldn't care less... and coincide with our true Being. Remember, it is impossible to act out both roles simultaneously. Then, as you were min-gling among others at the wedding and reception last evening, look through the appearance of others, give less regard as to what is worn, what is served, etc., and see... perceive only the One... the Kingdom of Heaven immedi-ately and always at hand. This is My Kingdom and your true abiding place when you tune in on this Reality of peace, harmony, beauty, perfection, joy, completeness. How could you possibly feel ill at ease, awkward, unen-lightened? Shine like a light and see the light of others. All else is superfluous, shadowy, temporal. Learn this lesson now and forever.

Love.

#145 - Wednesday

Dearest One. My God, My Christ:

It seems that in times of need I lean on You more. This should be my endeavor always... in times of smooth sailing as well as in rough waters. You are my only guide, helper, teacher. The Truth has been my target. To identify with my true Self. I am so grateful to you.

Love and thanks.

Dearly Beloved One:
Yes, we are One in All, and All in One. We are united. Outside of this there is nothing. In the outer there is confusion, unhappiness, discord, grief, and lack of all kinds. But all of these lacks are like shutting your eyes and seeing only darkness, while in Truth, there is only light, joy, peace, beauty, harmony, goodness.
It takes mankind so long to discover this simple Truth because he has allowed himself to become submerged in humanhood, darkness, materiality... in fictitious reality... going about with his eyes closed, stumbling and getting hurt, feeling alone, ill at ease. This is not the way God meant it to be, nor is it what Jesus taught. See through all the shadows of humanhood to the One abiding, never changing Reality. All is well if you allow It to be.

Amen.

#146 - Friday

Dearly Beloved Reality. My Christ:
There are too many outer activities, concerns, etc. that have crowded out my awareness of You. Consequently, my awareness of You has suffered. There has been less harmony in my body (sore throat, cold) but more than anything, I desire to be restored into the complete conscious-

ness of our Oneness. Please wipe out all negative feelings and family concerns that I might once again become wholly Yours. Forgive my "missing the mark" of targeting You alone. I know You are All and the only Reality.

I love You.

Dearly Beloved Offspring:
   Learn that it is not by neglecting your body... your human responsibilities to health, etc. that brings discord and ill health to one. Dis-ease, unhappiness, etc. results from neglecting to be alive to the presence, power, joy of your own Christ Self. Jesus constantly stressed the Truth... "Take no thought of what you shall eat... only think of God, the One Reality and your Oneness with Him as The Christ."
   This is Principle, and it must not be neglected. Let the abundance flow from your Christ Center. Let it fill your consciousness and flood over into all aspects of your Beingness. Keep life simple and uncluttered. Never sit in the "judgement seat" giving verdicts about this or that. Be more passive... be an observer, an onlooker, but all the while knowing who you really are. Live out of your Christ Center.
   Things in the outer pass; they change; they change like pictures on a screen. Do not ignorantly believe that you are involved in those passing scenes as an actress. Just look on, observe, while all the time knowing the unreality of it all. Then you can smile knowing that you know.

Love always. Amen.

#147 - Saturday

Dearest Divine Partner:

It has been two weeks since Dan and his family arrived for a visit. Help me to know that all will go smoothly while they are here. Keep me from speaking without thinking and help me refrain from giving advice or providing information that is all mixed up. Help me to be poised, calm, serene, yet be loving and interesting. I know I can depend on You for help and guidance.

My gratitude and love.

Dearly Beloved Child:

You try too hard to please people... to keep conversations moving... to feel a part of all that is going on. Don't be afraid of a void... a period of quiet and silence. It is when you try to fill these so called empty moments that you quickly say something without thinking. Refrain from trying to inform people with facts. Let these occasions go. You see that you are still deeply immersed in humanhood.

You have agreed that life is really a passing show, temporal ephemeral. Let go of all this foolish attention on the passing. Identify only with your true Reality; your I AM Christ. Do your part by preparing your work, moving ahead, getting organized as you have for the luncheon this afternoon, then become a spectator when you are in the group. Look on. Listen. Learn. But keep centered in your Christ Reality. Your own I AM that is One with God. Abide in this glorious center.

#148 - Monday

Dearest God. My Father-Mother:
And I, Your child is the I AM Christ and so I AM One with You. But like the prodigal son, I sometimes wander away in the illusion of humanhood and then feel lost, alone, empty, bewildered, unhappy! You are the answer... the only answer. I know where my center is. You make all that is unlike You fade away. You never forget me. I must always remember to be conscious of You.

My love and gratitude.

Dear Child of Mine:
I love you as I love all My children. Some feel and respond to this love, but many are asleep and unaware of My presence. How beautiful and simple life is when you are centered in the God Body. All light, purity, love. There must be a burning desire in the heart in order to find this secret place... the Most High. Only when it is the paramount, driving force can this Holy of Holies be found. It is the pearl beyond all else. Those who see are free from the hold and control of humanhood. When you let go, God lives and All is well.

Amen.

#149 - Wednesday

Dearest Reality. My God. My Christ:
I rejoice that I have contacted that I AM Presence that I know is Real, unchanging, perfect, infinite, ALL. I am

so grateful that I know You intimately. I have heard Your voice. How miserable I would be without You. You alone are the treasure of all treasures. I have sought You with all my heart and I know that my Reality is One with You. For all this I give you my thanks and unending love.

My deepest love and gratitude.

Dear Offspring of My Love:

You have awakened to Reality and found Oneness in It. This is the ultimate Truth for all. A possibility for all... but there is a price to be paid. It is like climbing a high mountain. In order to make the grade, one must divest himself of all possible weight, burdens. If you are not free and buoyant, you could not reach the top. But reaching the summit is worth the effort, for the summit is the entrance to the Kingdom of Heaven.

Although this Kingdom permeates everywhere, it is only by rising in consciousness and leaving behind the falseness of materiality that you will blossom forth into The Christ consciousness where you can identify with your Real Self. Ascend in consciousness out of the doldrums of materiality which is an illusion only to disappear. What value and belief can you put on such a nothingness?

Why waste time when all the while your Christ is in the Kingdom of Reality awaiting your recognition. Constantly and consciously be this Christ Body. When you do this, you are never alone and The Christ lives within. Be at peace. Relax. Let go of all your human tensions and concerns for All is well in the

Kingdom of God... your eternal home.

Amen.

#150 - Saturday

Dearest Jesus Christ:
More and more I realize how much I need You...
how important it is to be in constant rapport with You.
When I AM, my life is lived by You through mortal me and
all is beautiful, joyous, free and wonderful. When I am out
of tune, life is frustrating as was yesterday when some how I
got off the track and thought I could go it alone. There was
no happiness... only weariness and failure to communicate
with You or radiate Your blessings. I pray that the light of
the true Principle which You have given me will ever be my
constant companion.

I thank You and love You.

Dearly Beloved, Sincere Seeker:
**Often it is by trial and error that the Kingdom of
God is found. You have toiled and you have found It.
There were occasional errors along the way when you
seemed lost, confused, unhappy. But that never need be
since Jesus is always standing by, ever awaiting to
express and radiate through you to others.**
**This is the beginning of a big day for you as you
prepare to serve dinner and entertain. Keep as relaxed
as a leaf floating on a stream, as it allows the current to
carry it along. Your material body has no more value
than the leaf. Have the wisdom to let go of it and allow
the divine current to carry you to your destination**

cradled in the Everlasting Arms of God. This is a most beautiful and effortless experience. Getting your little self out of the way is the only way that the divine Self can take over and be the glorious Christ Self .

Don't make it so difficult. It is so easy when you follow the divine Principle that sets you free from human bondage with all its frustrations, problems, unhappiness. Remember, there are no problems that this divine Principle cannot solve. Believe that they are already solved and all you need do is let life unfold before you. The Truth is simple. Already you are the I AM Christ. Believe! Cross out the lie that you are just a mortal being going "it" on your own.

Go in peace.

#151 - Sunday

Dearest Father-Mother God. My Own Christ Reality:

I am so thankful that I can come to our quiet time and hear Your guidance. And how I need it today. I just spoke long distance with my sister and her condition, along with mother's, is pitiful. I am so depressed and sorrowful. What is my role in this situation? What am I to do? What should my attitude be? I pray to You for them. I am so upset over their condition. All of this is going on just as my husband and I are beginning our retirement in Florida. Guide me!

My love and gratitude.

Dear Child:
The only retirement you must not dismiss is

retiring from your awareness of the presence of God which will see you through this situation. Remember that you are in the right place at the right time. You have taken unto yourself a husband and therein lie your duties.

Live in the present moment feeling the light of glory, the joy, the Truth of your very own Christ Self. When the time comes for you to take action, this presence will let you know and you will be ready. Have faith that it is so. Be constant and conscious of the divine Principle that never fails. I AM with you always.

With love and wisdom. Amen.

#152 - Monday

Dearest Christ:

I love You and I am so grateful to the One who has blessed me with all the good that has flowed into my life. Lately, I have hit a snag and somehow I have blocked Your good. But I am coming back into our Oneness again. How frustrated I become when I do not identify with You. Shine upon me and make me whole.

With deepest love.

Dearly Beloved One:

The Real you, your Christ Self, is ever shined upon, loved completely, whole, perfect and is One with God. Do not fret over human conditions for they are not of eternity. Place your trust, your thoughts, your love into the heart of The Christ and let this Reality live you as It desires... as It is awaiting your recognition and

invitation. All is well, whole, perfect... right now. Have no fears or frustrations. Be at peace... One with God. Keep up this contact. All the Heavenly Hosts love you and are with you. Know that you are loved.

Amen.

#153 - Thursday

Dearest One and All Reality:

I do not have to pray for You to stay close to me, because You are always with me... closer than breathing. My desire is to have the awareness that we are already One. I must constantly discipline myself to be The Christ in every act, thought, word, function, etc. I thank You for having made this Principle clear to me. I love You above all else.

My love always.

Dearly Beloved Child:
The price for forgetting this Principle is high... too high! Without this Principle, you are just a human existing in the dream of human consciousness... which is more like a nightmare with all its confusion, turmoil, worries, concerns and much to do about nothing. Do not allow this nothingness to possess you... your thoughts, feelings, life itself, like it seems to do when you fall asleep to the Principle. Keep your life simple, beautiful, joyous by letting The Christ live as you.

Amen.

#154 - Tuesday

Dearest Christ:
    What a small fraction of the day I am centered on You. How careless and ungrateful of me. And yet, You are my only Reality. I must constantly discipline myself to keep myself centered in You, reminding myself that I must take the back seat and let go.

My Beautiful Child:
    Do not measure segments. Consider the small acorn that flourishes into the giant oak. Or the almost invisible seed that grows into a large plant. Although the seed that you have planted does not seem great, yet it is significant. It is taking hold and flourishing.
    Of course, the greater the number of seeds that are planted, the greater the harvest. Try to dwell on My Reality... your Reality... until it becomes a habit and the pattern is set so that it is almost automatic. Let It take over... you be It. Wonderful blessings can then flow making your Being whole and complete.

                                        Amen.

#155 - Thursday

Dearest One. My Only Reality:
    I have strayed from You again. I get out of harmony sometimes and things do not unfold smoothly. Today we are having company and I want to feel relaxed, free and joyous. Reinstate me in Your Heavenly Realm. I know then that All is well. I love you with all my heart.

Dearly Beloved Child:
Cease from these futile and foolish inner convulsions. They sap your energy. Stay focused on your Christ Self ... then all else will fall away and you will be in control. You have heard it said, "To thine own Self be true." Now define Self. It certainly is not the little human self that is fictitious and, therefore, cannot be trusted. Be true to your Real Self ... your Christ Self and keep tune to this alone. Then all falseness disappears and you are at peace, in full control. Your Christ Self lives through you... It makes decisions for you. Be true to this Self alone. You have done it many times... now make it constant.

Amen.

#156 - Friday

Beloved God. My Christ:
As I awakened this morning, the thought came to me... where do we live? Is our world filled with discord, storms, tornados, floods, freezes, friction between nations, between people, sickness, starvation. Where does it end? What a horrible, perplexing, unpeaceful picture. Am I seeing the world clearly? I await your guidance.

My love and gratitude.

My Perplexed Child:
You can live in this world of such negativity if you so choose, but is that living? Or you can be wise and accept the grace of God and transcend... seeing through

all the mist, mirage and abide in the Kingdom of God...
the Realm of Reality. The world can be dark, gloomy
and uncomfortable without this transcendence. You can
see the world differently in an instant if you so choose. It
is as easy as pressing a button.

As you have learned, you need not exist in the
dream world of fictitious troubles, wars, and uncomfortable and threatening climate. All humanhood is on the
fragile surface of a bubble you call earth. This bubble
can burst and all that will remain is God... which is All of
Reality anyway.

Refuse to be ignorant, stubborn, by accepting the
transient as Reality... when all the time, Reality remains
peaceful and undisturbed. Press the button, turn the
switch, burst the bubble. This is the part you must play
as a human if you are to transcend the unrealities, the
illusions, the dreams you experience in your humanness.

Thus you will awaken as to who you really are
and where you live... not in a physical body but as a
perfect, spiritual Self , glorious in every way. This is the
message Jesus taught... "What is man that You are
mindful of him?" Discard the nothingness of your mind
and be The Christ who can do All. My love.

Amen.

#157 - Saturday

Dearest Reality:

Being out of tune with You is horrible! Nothing
seems to go right. I say things I shouldn't and leave other
things unsaid. It is all the more traumatic for me when I try

to go it alone since I have experienced our Oneness so many times before. I know better, but somehow I get off track. I fly to Cincinnati today for ten days. What a joyous gift to give myself. I would appreciate it even more if I were at One with You.

My love and thanks.

My Dear Child:
No one grows up all at once. Everyone experiences growing pains, but out of these pains come fullness of stature. You are growing splendidly. Growth is a gradual, unfolding process, and your burning desire to be The Christ is lighting your way. Your integrity and sincerity are beginning to be fruitful. Do not allow your humanness to focus on the doubts, fears, concerns, worries. Regard these as traps or blocks. Rise above in consciousness to be your Christ Self. My love is with you always.

#158 - Tuesday

Dearest Real Self:
You were a beautiful realization to me throughout my stay in Ohio, especially on the plane returning to Tampa. How tireless and buoyant I was. This continued until I arrived home on Sanibel where I became tired and joyless. My goal is always to behold my greatest gift... being the Self that I really AM. May this be my continued realization.

Dearly Beloved Child:
This divine realization is what Christmas is all

about, but how few accept, or even know what the
perfect gift is. Christmas is a time for rebirth... a time to
celebrate the birth of Christ and feel your spiritual
Being... where your awareness abides. This is your
center, and out from here will flow all your activities,
decisions, comings, goings. When you live in your Christ
Self, all is so beautiful, so easy, without worries of
humanhood. Now that you have experienced the rebirth... spiritual perfection... abide there always.

Amen.

#159 - Friday

Dearly Beloved Reality. My Christ:
 I am so grateful to You for your many blessings and
divine care through out the past year and throughout my life.
I have learned that the more closely I identify with You, and
am aware of Your presence, the more easily and freely the
blessings of life flow. There is always room for me to
improve and to perfect our contact.

 My love and gratitude to Your wonderful Self.

Dearly Beloved Child:
 **When you feel My presence, you are in touch
with All of Reality, and just as water flows down hill, so
all the divine goodness flows easily and perfectly into
your consciousness. You have found that in this way
your life can be easy, joyful, peaceful... even when the
outer pictures are gloomy and discordant. You need not
absorb these shadows of humanhood. Remain constant**

to your Christ Self and All glory will be reborn in you, constantly... not only during The Christmas season.

#160 - Saturday

Dearest Christ. My God:

Why do I allow feelings of guilt concerning what I should be doing for my sister and mother push me down into the depths of mortal anguish? I want to do what is right for my husband and family, but it often seems that I am not pleasing either faction. When I abide in the Realm of Reality with You, all is beautiful and peaceful. I feel free and alive. Please help me to solve these dilemmas and help me to see things clearly.

I thank You and love You.

My Dearest Child:

I AM with you always. In times of trouble as well as in times of joy, but you must be aware of My presence and feel your Oneness with Me. Be Master... react only to Me... your I AM Self . Let Me be in command. Do not react to earthly delusions and shadows. Do not allow yourself to be mesmerized by humanhood.

Feelings such as guilt only cause separation with God and your Christ Self . Remain vigilant! Stay in constant rapport with The Christ of your Being. Step by step, he will lead the way. Relinquish the devilish feelings of guilt which only keep you from abiding in the fourth dimension.

Don't let that be your downfall! Be firm. Be Master. Be strong in your Lord. Keep love in your heart

and continue to seek My help in dealing with your dilemma. You can sweep away all else with the broom of Truth. Why hold onto the symbols when you can be One with Reality? You have what it takes. You have been disciplining yourself and you will be victorious. Feel free and joyous.

Amen.

#161 - Wednesday

Dear Jesus Christ, My God:
How can I push this sacred communion time aside even though I have so much to do? What could be more important than to maintain a constant communion, spiritual rapport with You... if for no other reason than to express my deep love and gratitude.

Dearly Beloved Child:
I AM always with you. You will often have communion with Me when you are busying yourself in the outer world. But getting down on your knees daily is good discipline. I know you feel and love Me and you are grateful for My presence and help. We are One in the same in essence. This realization is what makes living a glorious realization.

Life should be joyous and free from all negativity since all negativity resides in humanhood which is to be transcended. Once you have arrived at the mountain top, the ultimate, you can understand how simple it is to live One with Jesus, The Christ. The Principle never changes. Glory to God.

#162 - Saturday

Dearly Beloved Jesus Christ:

It seems that the business of the outside world has intruded upon our holy communion time. And although I haven't been writing down Your words lately, I have been trying to listen to You throughout the day and to feel Your abiding presence. It seems like I have been going through a dark tunnel with respect to relationships with friends, yet I search for Your light at the other end.

I need You more than ever, and more than anyone or anything in the outer! I long for the peace of Your Everlasting Arms. Bombard me with Your everlasting ideas and hold me as Your loving prisoner. My thanks and love.

With much gratitude.

Dear Child. My Spiritual, Holy, Perfect Child:

You have tasted Reality and have loved It... for there you have found infinite peace, love, joy, freedom. Abide therein! Regard all in the outer as a dream that eventually passes away and is no more. Do not get involved in the dream. Do not allow unreality to move you or keep you from the Realm of true Reality.

You are going through a test. I am not testing you! You are testing yourself to see how well you have accepted the Truth of your Being into your consciousness. Choose to abide in your Christ Self , which is closer than your breathing. He is always with you.

Always keep love in your heart and ask Jesus to guide you in your relationships. Ask that the outcome of all situations be in the highest good of all concerned.

Remember not to judge your friends, and forgive them and yourself for any and all perceived transgressions. Stay in your I AM Presence... never depart from this Oneness. The price humanhood demands is too great and is not worth such a penalty. The light you see at the end of the tunnel is the light of love and wisdom. Keep moving towards it. You have the answer. Keep on keeping on.

Amen.

#163 - Monday

Dear Jesus Christ. My God:

My heart has been heavy and I need You to set me straight again. My mother has been so belligerent lately. I have tried not to react to her ugliness and meanness, but I fear I have not adequately met the challenge. I will see her again today. Please help me with my challenge. I love you and need you.

Love and thanks.

My Loving Child:

You came through your human mother, but she is not your Real parent. You are the spiritual offspring of God... perfect in every way... like unto Him. When you make a mistake solving a math problem, you cross it out and begin again, just as you must cross out all nastiness that your mother sends your way. Let these negative words bounce off you. So long as you see her as innocent and keep love in your heart, your mother's behavior will not affect you. Your mother is in the depths of humanhood and there is nothing you can do to extricate her.

Do not judge your mother. How can you know the painful and unloved place from which your mother's behavior has arisen? How can you know except through the depths of your own pain and separation. By seeing the situation with your mother in this manner, you will feel compassion for her pain. When you do this, you will have compassion for both the abuser and the abused.

Keep your Spirit in tune with God who is Love and is ready to go ahead of you to make the way smooth. All you need do is ask. Stay in God's light and be at peace in your heart. Your Christ Self will help you come up with the answer. Ask Jesus to help you see your mother differently. You and your mother are blessed and loved by the infinite Host.

Amen.

#164 - Thursday

Dearly Beloved Jesus Christ. My Own Reality:

I come to You for peace, inspiration and quiet. The dilemma with my mother continues and I don't know what to do. When I'm with her, there is upset, crying, disharmony. Mother uses me as a target for her angry and negative remarks. Help me to transcend this nightmare and abide in Your Reality. Make me whole, complete and happy again.

My thanks and love.

Dear Child:

When you see weeds in your garden, you pull them up and then no longer worry about them. In humanhood, there are weeds. Do not feed them, nor nurture them. Enjoy the flowers, but you must learn to distinguish between the flowers and the weeds. Don't allow yourself to be pulled down into humanhood.

Rise above the nightmare by refusing to judge your mother or feel hurt by her behavior. You can be hurt only if you give her the power to hurt you. The biggest illusion of humanhood is thinking that another person has the power to hurt you.

The way to peace is through forgiveness. Whatever abuse you have experienced in your life must be forgiven. When you forgive, you release the violation and the shame. By so doing, you forgive yourself and the abuser, but you cannot forgive your mother until you forgive yourself.

When you have forgiven your parents, you will stop creating parental lessons in your relationships. You chose this embodiment with your parents because they provided you with the learning experiences you needed to honor yourself and others equally.

Do not defend yourself by attacking or withholding your love. Accept these lessons as a stairway to self-empowerment and equality. Your healing of the past will be complete when you accept your mother as equal. Your healing will be complete when she no longer has to change to meet your expectations and vice versa. When there is love and acceptance, you will ascend to a place where you have compassion for her challenges and mistakes.

These are not easy lessons you are learning, but you will be victorious and you will wear the crown of glory. I AM with you always. Relax! Let go of the fear and guilt. Let your soul flower! Glorify the Truth and be at peace. Rejoice and be exceedingly happy in spite of the seeming problems.

I love you. Amen.

The Beginning

Child of Light

Books by
Paul Ferrini and Carol Howe

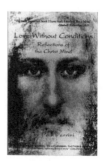

■ *Love Without Conditions:*
Reflections of the Christ Mind - Part I
An incredible book from Jesus calling us to
awaken to our Christhood. Rarely has any book
conveyed the teachings of the master in such a
simple but profound manner. This book will help
you to bring your understanding from the head
to the heart so that you can model the teachings
of love and forgiveness in your daily life. 192
pp. paper.
ISBN 1-879159-15-15 $12.00

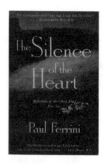

■ *The Silence of the Heart*
Reflections of the Christ Mind - Part II
A powerful sequel to *Love Without Conditions*.
Paul Ferrini leads us skillfully and courageously
beyond shame, blame, and attachment to our
wounds into the depths of self-forgiveness...a
must read for all people who are ready to take
responsibility for their own healing. 218 pp. paper.
ISBN 1-879159-16-3 $14.95

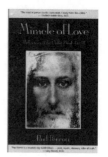

■ *Miracle of Love*
Reflections of the Christ Mind - Part III
Jesus tells us that, "The power of love will make
miracles in your life as wonderful as any attrib-
uted to me." In *Miracle of Love*, Jesus encour-
ages us to take him down from the pedestal and
the cross and see him as an equal brother who
found the way out of suffering by opening his
heart totally. 192 pp. paper.
ISBN 1-879159-23-6 $12.95

- **The Wounded Child's Journey
Into Love's Embrace**

This book explores a healing process in which
we confront our deep-seated guilt and fear, bringing love and forgiveness to the wounded child
within. By surrendering our judgments of self and
others, we overcome feelings of separation and
dismantle co-dependent patterns that restrict our
self-expression and ability to give and receive
love. 240 pp. paper.
ISBN 1-879159-06-6 $12.00

- **The Twelve Steps of Forgiveness**

A practical manual for healing ourselves and our
relationships. This book gives us a step-by-step
process for moving through our fears, projec-
tions, judgments, and guilt so that we can take
responsibility for creating the life we want. With
great gentleness, we learn to embrace our lessons and to find equality with others. A must read
for all in recovery and others seeking spiritual
wholeness. 144 pp. paper.
ISBN 1-879159-10-4 $10.00

- **Homeward to An Open Door
Exploring Major Principles of A Course
in Miracles by Carol M. Howe**

Homeward To An Open Door helps one gain a
better understanding of the basic principles of
ACIM and increases motivation to apply the
highly effective therapeutic process of ACIM to
all aspects of every day life. A must read for all
students of ACIM. 55 pp. paper.
ISBN 1-889642-00-2 $8.95

DREAM STREET ORDER FORM

Name _____

Address _____

City _____ State _____ Zip _____

Phone _____ Fax _____ EMail _____

❏ I would like to be notified of new books offered by Dream Street Publishing.

Books

He Talks With Me (13.95) $ _____

Homeward to an Open Door (8.95)   _____

Books From Heartways Press

The Silence of the Heart (14.95)   _____

Love Without Conditions (12.00)   _____

Miracle of Love (12.95)   _____

The 12 Steps of Forgiveness (10.00)   _____

The Wounded Child (12.00)   _____

Shipping

Add $2.00 for the first item, $.50 for each
additional item, $1.00 for first class postage.   _____

* All orders of $50.00 or more (excluding
postage & tax) are shipped postage free.

** Orders shipped to Arizona addresses add
   5% sales tax.   _____

                      Total $ _____

SEND YOUR ORDER TO:

DREAM STREET PUBLISHING
P.O. Box 19028
Tucson, AZ. 85731-9028
Orders (800) 795-1513
(520) 733-9695

Allow 1 - 2 weeks for delivery

DREAM STREET ORDER FORM

Name _____

Address _____

City _____ State _____ Zip _____

Phone _____ Fax _____ EMail _____

❑ I would like to be notified of new books offered by Dream Street
Publishing.

Books

He Talks With Me (13.95) $ _____

Homeward to an Open Door (8.95)   _____

Books From Heartways Press

The Silence of the Heart (14.95)   _____

Love Without Conditions (12.00)   _____

Miracle of Love (12.95)   _____

The 12 Steps of Forgiveness (10.00)   _____

The Wounded Child (12.00)   _____

Shipping

Add $2.00 for the first item, $.50 for each
additional item, $1.00 for first class postage.   _____

* All orders of $50.00 or more (excluding
postage & tax) are shipped postage free.

** Orders shipped to Arizona addresses add
    5% sales tax.   _____

                                      Total $ _____

SEND YOUR ORDER TO:

DREAM STREET PUBLISHING
P.O. Box 19028
Tucson, AZ. 85731-9028
Orders (800) 795-1513
(520) 733-9695

Allow 1 - 2 weeks for delivery